Cambridge Elements ☰

Elements in World Englishes
edited by
Edgar W. Schneider
University of Regensburg

T0287076

UNIFORMITY AND VARIABILITY IN THE INDIAN ENGLISH ACCENT

Caroline R. Wiltshire
University of Florida

CAMBRIDGE
UNIVERSITY PRESS

CAMBRIDGE
UNIVERSITY PRESS

University Printing House, Cambridge CB2 8BS, United Kingdom

One Liberty Plaza, 20th Floor, New York, NY 10006, USA

477 Williamstown Road, Port Melbourne, VIC 3207, Australia

314–321, 3rd Floor, Plot 3, Splendor Forum, Jasola District Centre,
New Delhi – 110025, India

79 Anson Road, #06–04/06, Singapore 079906

Cambridge University Press is part of the University of Cambridge.

It furthers the University's mission by disseminating knowledge in the pursuit of
education, learning, and research at the highest international levels of excellence.

www.cambridge.org
Information on this title: www.cambridge.org/9781108823272
DOI: 10.1017/9781108913768

First published 2020

A catalogue record for this publication is available from the British Library.

ISBN 978-1-108-82327-2 Paperback
ISSN 2633-3309 (online)
ISSN 2633-3295 (print)

Additional resources for this publication at www.cambridge.org/wiltshire

Cambridge University Press has no responsibility for the persistence or accuracy of
URLs for external or third-party internet websites referred to in this publication
and does not guarantee that any content on such websites is, or will remain,
accurate or appropriate.

Uniformity and Variability in the Indian English Accent

Elements in World Englishes

DOI: 10.1017/9781108913768
First published online: November 2020

Caroline R. Wiltshire
University of Florida

Author for correspondence: Caroline R. Wiltshire, wiltshir@ufl.edu

Abstract: The sounds of Indian English are distinct and recognizable to outsiders, while insiders perceive variations in how English has developed in this large diverse population. What characteristics mark the unity? Which are clues to a speaker's origins or identity? This Element synthesizes research over the past fifty years and adds to it, focusing on selected features of consonants, vowels, and suprasegmentals (stress, intonation, rhythm) to understand the characteristics of Indian English accents and sources of its uniformity and variability. These accent features, perceptible by humans and discoverable by computational approaches, may be used in expressing identity, both local and pan-Indian.

Keywords: Indian English, dialect variation, accents, second language acquisition, language contact

ISBNs: 9781108823272 (PB), 9781108913768 (OC)
ISSNs: 2633-3309 (online), 2633-3295 (print)

Contents

1 Introduction

India may have the second largest population of English speakers in the world, with over 122 million citizens of India describing themselves as speakers of English in the 2011 Census. The codification of the sound system of "Indian English" as a distinct variety began approximately fifty years ago (CIEFL 1972, Kachru 1983, Bansal & Harrison 2013 [1972]), and continues to this day (Sailaja 2009, Pandey 2015). However, descriptions of the phonetics and phonology of Indian English (IndE) reveal a tension between perhaps aspirational portrayals of IndE as a unified accent with a single set of norms vs. detailed descriptions of varieties of English in India based primarily on the first languages (L1s) of the speakers (e.g., Nagarajan 1985, Jose 1992, Wiltshire & Harnsberger 2006). There are also occasional claims of regional variations (Gargesh 2004) and commonalities (Wiltshire 2005, Wiltshire 2015).

Studies on variation within IndE have documented differences in terms of consonant and vowel inventories, allophonics, phonotactics, and suprasegmentals like stress, intonation, and rhythm. On the other hand, recent research suggests that IndE, especially that of educated urban speakers, has been converging toward a more homogeneous standard. Maxwell and Fletcher (2009: 66) claim that "that there are a range of shared vowel categories across speakers of IndE of different L1 backgrounds," based on comparing results from Hindi and Punjabi L1 speakers with those from speakers of other L1 backgrounds, such as Tamil and Gujarati (Wiltshire & Harnsberger 2006). Sirsa and Redford (2013) found both segmental and prosodic similarities among speakers of two different L1s, Hindi and Telugu, summarizing their results as largely consistent with their hypothesis that IndE has phonological targets distinct from those of Indian languages.

This Element explores questions of what unites IndE accents across the nation, what distinguishes subvarieties, and, to the extent possible, what are the sources of these accent features. As English in India, like English everywhere, has developed through contact and over time, theories of language development (e.g., Mufwene 2001, Schneider 2003, 2007, Trudgill 2004) suggest sources of both uniformity and variability may be found through an examination of founder varieties, substrates, linguistic markedness, and processes such as dialect leveling, koineization, and focusing. I begin with an overall description of the linguistic situation in India and English's place in it, along with discussions of the object of study ("IndE accent") and potential factors involved in its development (Section 2). I then combine the findings of acoustic studies, including my own, on IndE sounds, from consonants and vowels through suprasegmentals (Sections 3–5), evaluating possible unifying and distinguishing characteristics and their sources. In Section 6, I report on the ability of IndE speakers and computational analyses to perceive variation within IndE, and speakers' attitudes toward variation and identity, before discussing the overall findings and areas for future research in Section 7.

2 Linguistic Situation in India

I first provide brief descriptions of the range of languages used in India (Section 2.1), the current status of English (Section 2.2), the meanings of the term "Indian English" and its use in this Element (Section 2.3), and potential sources of uniformity and variability in the development of English in India (Section 2.4).

2.1 Languages in India

India is home to a large number of languages (Figure 1); the 2011 Census listed 121 languages with over 10,000 native speakers each (Government of India 2011), while Ethnologue[1] lists a total of 447 living languages.

The vast majority of languages fall into four distinct language families: Indo-Aryan (originally from the West), Dravidian (always in India), Tibeto-Burman, and Austroasiatic (both from the East). Most of India's population speaks an Indo-Aryan or Dravidian language as their L1 (see Table 1 for examples). Although historically unrelated to each other, languages from the Indo-Aryan and Dravidian families have been in contact for millennia; many have come to share linguistic features, leading to descriptions of India as a "Linguistic Area" (Emeneau 1956, Masica 1976). However, the Tibeto-Burman languages, spoken in the northeast of the country and relatively isolated from the rest of India, are phonologically and phonetically quite distinct. For example, most Tibeto-Burman languages lack retroflex consonants but have phonemic tone, while Indo-Aryan and Dravidian languages generally have retroflex consonants and lack tone. Assamese, genetically an Indo-Aryan language, is in close proximity with Tibeto-Burman languages and shares some characteristics with its neighbors, including a lack of retroflexion.

Table 1 provides background about the distribution of eighteen languages in India, with the number of speakers reporting each as a "mother tongue" (L1) from the 2011 census (Government of India 2011); these specific languages are chosen because they are referred to in the research below. This census also asked speakers to report any second or third languages, and for the L1s here I have included the number who reported English as an L2/L3.

---

[1] www.ethonologue.com/country/IN. Accessed 2020/1/16.

Figure 1 States and union territories of India by the most commonly spoken L1[2]

All numbers are self-reports and may be problematic in a variety of ways (Kohli 2017 provides a good critique). For example, it is unclear what speakers mean when describing a language as their "mother tongue"; it may be the language of their mother, whether or not the respondent speaks it best or first. There is no provision for indicating level of competence or amount of use for any of the languages listed. Those listing English as L2/L3 may range widely in both: at one extreme, people who attended English-medium schools from pre-kindergarten and currently use English daily with friends and work-colleagues, and at the other, people who grew up with a different language and first encountered English as a school subject at age twelve or later, with little use for it after leaving school.

The census calculated overall rates of bilingualism (26 per cent) and trilingualism (7.1 per cent) of the population (Government of India 2011), both of which are surely too low. Sridhar (1989) suggests reasons for the

---

[2] https://commons.wikimedia.org/w/index.php?curid=51479325

Table 1 Number of speakers of L1s and those knowing English (Government of India 2011).

Family	Language	Primarily spoken in	Number of L1 speakers	Number of English L2	Number of English L3
Indo-European	English	Throughout	259,578	76,578,017	45,554,093
Dravidian	Kannada	Karnataka	43,706,512	3,450,332	962,147
	Malayalam	Kerala	34,838,819	6,728,063	890,036
	Tamil	Tamil Nadu	69,026,881	12,325,941	783,805
	Telugu	Andhra Pradesh	81,127,740	8,074,805	2,900,566
Indo-Aryan	Assamese	Assam	15,311,351	984,983	748,554
	Bangla	West Bengal	97,237,669	4,710,845	1,812,485
	Gujarati	Gujarat	55,492,554	937,868	6,752,677
	Hindi	UP, MP	528,347,193	32,018,890	3,238,254
	Marathi	Maharashtra	83,026,680	1,395,659	10,220,047
	Oriya/Odia	Odisha	37,521,324	4,879,878	2,045,591
	Punjabi	Punjab	33,124,726	2,036,498	7,828,657
Tibeto-Burman	Angami/Tenyidie	Nagaland	152,796	62,322	11,833
	Ao	Nagaland	260,008	71,657	21,604
	Meitei/Manipuri	Manipur	1,761,079	480,817	108,473
	Mizo/Lushai	Mizoram	830,846	149,076	7,247
	Bodo (Boro)	Assam	1,482,929	31,991	38,584
Austroasiatic	Khasi	Meghalaya	1,431,344	237,173	16,944

underreporting: "speakers are reluctant to claim competence in a language unless they can read and write it; many languages are traditionally regarded simply as dialects of one of the major languages of the region; competence in a non-prestigeful language is not considered worth mentioning" (1989: 2). The final point raises the possibility that speakers will claim English as an L2/L3 regardless of their level of competence or use, as it is generally considered prestigious. Nonetheless, Table 1 illustrates that percentages of speakers reporting English as an L2/L3 varies widely based on L1 and region. Although the overall average is about 10 per cent, L1 Malayalam, Angami, Ao, and Manipuri speakers average over 20 per cent, while Bengali, Hindi, and Bodo speakers average under 7 per cent.

The national language of India is Hindi, though the constitution designates English as a co-official language. States have generally been designed along linguistic lines, and may choose their own languages for official status along with the national languages Hindi and English. Thus Gujarati is the official language of Gujarat, Telugu of Andhra Pradesh, and so on. However, some states, especially those with a great deal of internal linguistic diversity such as Nagaland, chose (Indian) English as an official state language and regional lingua franca. Other states list English as one of their official languages, including Meghalaya, Goa, and Tripura, and many list it as an "additional official language" (Haryana, Karnataka, Mizoram, etc.). Although English plays a role in government, businesses, and schools across India, the rise in English has not led to widespread language shift (Sahgal 1991: 300); instead English provides an additional resource in the multilingual repertoire of its users. Over 99 per cent of Indians list an Indian language as their L1, and few, approximately 0.02 per cent, list English. Nonetheless, English has been described as "a major player in the language ecology of contemporary India" (Sridhar 1989: xiv), so I turn now to its place within India.

2.2 English in India

English was introduced to India by the British, beginning in the 1600s; for more detail on its past, see the overviews provided in Schneider (2007), Mukherjee (2007), and Sharma (2017). The term 'British' encompasses a wide range of varieties, including not only the most prestigious standard forms in England, but also regional and social dialects, along with other British varieties such as Scottish, Welsh, and Irish. Bernaisch and Koch (2016) point out that even Americans had a small presence in the early days of colonization. The potential effects of these varieties on the development of IndE are discussed further in Section 2.4.

Currently English performs a range of public functions as the language of the national legislature, the legal system, and some state governments, as well as being widely used in business and higher education, especially in the sciences, medicine, and technology (Sailaja 2009). English is primarily used with other Indian speakers of English, rather than outsiders, and Kachru (1976) observes that in India "the English language is used to 'integrate' culturally and linguistically pluralistic societies. 'Integration' with the British or American culture is not the primary aim" (1976: 229). More recently, Mallikarjun (2020: 166) reaffirms that the primary motivation for learning English continues to be for use as a lingua franca inside India, not with external speakers. English use in India is largely an urban rather than rural phenomenon, and the concentration of the population into urban centers has been increasing over the past six decades (Kohli 2017: 31). Kohli further notes that the urban vs. rural division correlates with privilege, including opportunities to learn and use English, and Agnihotri and Khanna (1997) commented that "those who form their impressions based on their experiences in Bombay and Delhi are likely to have a misleading picture of the use of English in India" (1997: 70). Furthermore, use of English is more common in the public domain than the private. Agnihotri and Khanna's survey of 1,128 urban users of English reported home use as only 36 per cent on average, although it also showed that "in urban metropolitan India, English is making serious claims as a language of peer group communication" (1997: 67).

While English is not widely replacive of Indian languages, nor widely used as a home language, two journalists over the past decade have described a relatively new phenomenon in which English is both. In mixed marriages in urban settings, English has become the home language and the L1 for children in those homes, according to Rai (2012) and Pai (2018). Rai describes communities in Bangalore, where she writes that a "generation of urban children is growing up largely monolingual – speaking, thinking and dreaming only in English." Pai (2018) similarly reports on a new "caste" based primarily on advanced English skills, a group she describes as "affluent, urban, highly-educated, usually in intercaste or inter-religious unions." The size of this emerging group is quite small; even Pai estimates that only the top 1 per cent of people who use English in India fall into this group, which may be the same small subset of the urban population Krishnaswamy and Burde (1998: 127) described as having lost their mother tongue and cultural roots in favor of English. However, even the top 1 per cent of English users in India means over a million people, and as both urban populations and mixed marriages rise, this is a phenomenon to monitor.

As for popular culture, English has made only small inroads into movies, music, and the performing arts (Sailaja 2009), but has successfully increased its presence in both publishing and TV since the opening of the economy in the early 1990s (Sailaja 2009, Chand 2010, Kohli 2017). Kohli (2017: 34–35) documents the presence of English in published media, with a thriving English newspaper industry and a third-place ranking, after only the USA and the UK, in English book publishing. Furthermore, Kohli (2017: 35) observes that "English also has a powerful and growing presence in Indian television and cable news channels some of which provide round-the-clock programs," while Chand (2010) writes that "Cable TV channels based in India, e.g. NDTV, have been influential in de-stigmatizing various non-RP Indian accents through talk shows and other programs in IndE" (2010: 25).

Although media exemplifies a range of accents to Indian users of English, it is the choice of pedagogical model that has garnished the most attention from academics. As English came to India with the British, the presumed model had been some form of British English (BrE) for generations, and many teachers were foreigners. Since the late 1960s, however, there has been a movement toward using a more local English model (CIEFL 1972, Bansal & Harrison 2013[1972], Nihalani et al. 1979). Nihalani, Tongue, and Hosali claim "this view that the only suitable model for Indian learners is British Received Pronunciation is not shared by the majority of the people in the country, not even by many distinguished teachers of English" (1979: 204). Newer models were prescribed, based on descriptions of English as spoken by proficient speakers from around India, with the explicit goal of devising a form of English that serves as "a socially acceptable pronunciation devoid of regional peculiarities" (Pandey 1981: 11). The principle behind such models of English have been accepted to the extent that currently, English teachers in India are primarily speakers of a local English.

The development of a local model belongs in Stage 4 of the Schneider (2003, 2007) model of Postcolonial English development. This stage, "endonormative stabilization," accompanies political and psychological independence, where-upon a local variety of English begins to be seen as an expression of a new and independent identity. These developments should foster an increased accept-ance of the local English, as the "existence of a new language form is recognized and this form has lost its former stigma and is positively evaluated" (Schneider 2007: 50). An increasingly positive attitude toward IndE within India has been documented over the last four decades, from Kachru (1976) to Bernaisch and Koch (2016).

Kachru (1976) reports on a large-scale survey of 700 students in BA/MA programs, 196 English college/university teachers, and 29 heads of English Departments. These respondents ranked BrE as their preferred teaching model (averaging 66.7 per cent for faculty, 67.6 per cent for students), well over IndE (26.7 per cent, 22.7 per cent), although more reported that they themselves speak IndE (55.6 per cent overall). Approximately fifteen years later, Sahgal (1991) surveyed 45 speakers in elite areas of Delhi, and their choice of model showed a large swing to a preference for "ordinary Indian English" (47 per cent) over others, including the English of AIR/TV (All-India Radio/TV) announcers (27 per cent) as "it was felt by some of my informants that AIR/TV announcers imitated the BBC pronunciation and had not evolved their own identity" (Sahgal 1991: 304). Sahgal summarized the results as showing both increased awareness of IndE and more acceptance of its distinct norms. Shortly thereafter (1993–4), Agnihotri and Khanna conducted their large (n = 1128) urban survey, finding English-medium education more widespread in the younger generation, which claims higher levels of proficiency and more positive attitudes toward both English and English-speaking Indians (Agnihotri & Khanna 1997: 98). Furthermore, "English is perceived as one of the Indian languages by nearly 75 per cent of the informants in this study" (Agnihotri & Khanna 1997: 90).

Later surveys continue to elicit answers that some form of BrE is the best teaching model (Hohenthal 2003, Padwick 2010), yet show positive attitudes toward IndE, especially for use within India. Hohenthall's thirty participants agreed overall with statements like "I like speaking English" (80 per cent yes) and "English is important to India as a whole" (90 per cent yes), while 55 per cent of Padwick's fifty participants chose IndE, when asked which variety should be spoken in India, over second place "don't know/mind" (21 per cent). As pointed out in Bernaisch and Koch (2016), even the choice of a different model for the classroom does not mean that the participants lack a positive attitude toward their own English. Bernaisch and Koch (2016) found positive attitudes toward IndE in their survey that asked participants to rate how well thirteen words pairs, related to competence, power, solidarity, and status, characterized IndE, BrE, AmE, and Sri Lankan English. Based on ninety-four responses from highly-educated urban participants, the overall results show positive attitudes toward all varieties. Though BrE is rated higher on most categories, IndE rates higher on solidarity attributes 'friendly' and 'humble', suggesting covert prestige. Bernaisch and Koch also found that young women both use IndE structures and have the most positive attitudes toward IndE, and, as women often lead linguistic change, they suggest that positive attitudes would continue to grow among IndE speakers.

These studies indicate a growing awareness and acceptance of local IndE as playing a role in India, with at least covert prestige but continued mixed feelings about the choice of a model. Issues of model choice may also relate to how English in India is perceived: as a unified goal or as a set of acceptable varieties, an issue to which I now turn.

2.3 "Indian English" as a Variety/Set of Varieties

In Schneider's (2003, 2007) dynamic model, English in India has likely passed stage 3, "nativisation," in which "the shape of English is a strongly localized one, a characteristic which is due to some extent to the fact that learners have approximated not inaccessible external models but rather local ones" (2007: 167), and entered stage 4 "endonormative stabilization," in which the localized norms provide the target for acquisition. Stabilization is normally followed by differentiation among varieties, whether regional or social in stage 5, although Schneider (2003) warns that the ideal of homogeneity at stage 4 is usually somewhat mythical. Mukherjee (2007) argues that "the situation in which Indian English finds itself today could be seen as a stable, productive steady state in the evolutionary process in which there is an equilibrium between conflicting forces of progression and conservativism" (2007: 157), mixing some stage 3 traits (complaint tradition) with some of stage 5 (heterogeneity developed and developing).

An "Indian English accent" is easily recognized, both by foreigners and IndE speakers (Bush 1967, Bansal 1976, Chand 2009, McCullough 2013, Fuchs 2015), suggesting that there are characteristics that distinguish it as a whole from other varieties of English. Bush (1967) found that her twelve AmE listeners correctly identify IndE words and sentences when presented with clear speech samples from four speakers each of AmE (Midwest), BrE (RP), and IndE (L1 Hindi from U.P.). These same listeners were not as accurate distinguishing between AmE and BrE samples. McCullough (2013) showed that even very short samples, a consonant-vowel sequence, were enough for her twenty-eight AmE listeners to distinguish IndE from the other English accents presented (AmE, Korean, Mandarin). Fuchs (2015) created versions of a three-sentence recording from BrE and IndE speakers, manipulated to contain only certain cues (segmental, pitch, rhythm), and asked listeners (17IndE, 17BrE) to judge the speech as British/somewhat British/somewhat Indian/Indian. Both types of listeners clearly distinguished the accents, and all types of cues influenced their decisions, with segmental cues being the most important. These studies all suggest that there are qualities that contribute to the common perception of an accent as IndE. Additionally, while users of IndE have long reported that they can distinguish varieties within IndE and even guess where the speaker is from, there is now some evidence that speakers of IndE can distinguish at least among Northern, Southern, and Northeastern varieties of IndE (Sirsa & Redford 2013, Sitaram et al. 2018, Chakraborty & Didla 2020; see Section 6.1 for further discussion).

Given the potential uniformity and variability, opinions range widely about the proper use of the term "Indian English" and its relationship to variation.

Some use "Indian English" as the name for a particular kind of English from which other varieties deviate, others use it as an umbrella term for the whole set of varieties spoken in India, and still others argue that there is no use for the term because there is only "English in India," not "Indian English." After reviewing some of these positions, I also describe which Indian English this Element examines for potentially relevant characteristics.

Early writings are oriented toward promulgating a standard, with variations of English spoken in India treated as substandard in some way, often as learners' errors or fossilizations falling short of the "target." Such works attempt to identify an "educated Indian English" to treat as a model, sometimes justified as the most likely to be intelligible (e.g., Bansal 1976, Bansal & Harrison 2013 [1972]). It is not always clear whether this "educated" version actually exists; for example, CIEFL (1972: 15–16) provides a long prescriptive list of potential difficulties based on sixteen L1 backgrounds and marks speakers of all back-grounds as having problems with some of their recommended standards. Bansal and Harrison (2013 [1972]: 4), on the other hand, claim that "in every region there are people who have shaken off the gross features of regional accent and speak a more 'neutral' form of Indian English." Pandey (2015) seems to take this viewpoint as well when he writes, "English-medium education as well as higher education has helped reduce the variation to the extent that a more general variety has emerged as an acceptable standard across the subcontinent" (2015: 301). Thus, from this perspective, there is a model IndE accent, and only a lack of proper education or successful learning contributes to variation. Domange (2015) objects that seeing variation only as the result of incomplete learning ignores the range of factors involved in normal varietal development: "IE varieties are not conceptualised as emerging from interaction between the speakers, let alone as developing from one generation to the next" (2015: 535).

The term "Indian English" has also widely been seen as a term covering a whole range of varieties. For example, Chand (2009: 307) writes that "Indian English is an umbrella term for multiple English varieties spoken in India by speakers of varying fluency, nativity, ethnic, regional, and linguistic back-grounds." Sharma (2017) also notes that it is useful as an "umbrella term" for related varieties, and claims that although the term Indian English is generally used to refer to an acrolectal style, "certainly no single variety or standard is shared across the North or the South, much less across the entire country" (2017: 326), raising the possibility that there is more than one acrolectal variety, based on geographical or social factors. As a version of the umbrella viewpoint, "Indian English" may be a cover term for specific characteristics that are shared across varieties, which seems to be the position of Nihalani et al. (1979) when they suggest that "Indian English, in spite of all the variety that one notices from one linguistic group to another, from one region to another, and even from one speaker to another, retains a fairly uniform pattern" (1979: 228). Similarly Bansal (1983) predicted that, despite claims of rampant dialectal variation, particularly in accents, "[i]t will be found, however, that, in spite of all the diversity, the linguistic system is fairly uniform even in a heterogeneous community like the Indian speakers of English" (1983: 34). More recently, Maxwell and Fletcher (2010) observe that research indicates "English spoken in India demonstrates a number of features that are shared by speakers across the subcontinent" (2010: 28). These shared patterns or features may be the source of uniformity that defines an "Indian English Accent."

Finally, Kohli (2017) argues that there is no "Indian English" per se, only Englishes used in India (or Bharat) by a variety of speakers in a variety of contexts, so that claims of a unified entity to be called Indian English are premature at best. As sources of variation, she points to the many kinds of diversity in India: economic, social, religious, linguistic, geographic, and educational, and notes that, even for its most fluent speakers, English is only one of their linguistic resources, which means that English plays different roles in their lives depending on the domains appropriate for their other languages. Instead of presuming that there is an Indian English, she recommends that research proceed by describing local varieties of specific communities and speakers, which can then be compared to determine if there are in fact characteristics in common. Kohli is focused on grammatical aspects other than pronunciation, and argues that widely accepted standards in the grammatical system of English around the world prevent extensive Indianization. This may be true for the non-phonological grammar and yet still be compatible with the idea that accent allows for new standards that can be used for local identities, just as other standard Englishes allow for diverse accents.

So what counts as *an* IndE accent, and what could count as *the* IndE accent? If we ask the same of AmE or BrE accents, clearly the answer is not simple. There are overtly prestigious accents, but even the media and dictionary guides to pronunciation allow for variation among acceptable accents, both social and regional. If we try to distill features that are common within one variety and distinctive from the other (flapping in AmE vs. BrE, non-rhoticity in BrE vs. AmE), we find exceptions (Liverpool BrE has flaps, Boston AmE is non-rhotic). Sailaja (2009) makes the same point when writing "It is important to note that there are no monolithic varieties of English in UK or USA … India is no different. Just as there are varieties of British English, there are varieties of Indian English as well." (2009: 14). Mohanan (1992) proposes that the methods for describing the phonology of non-native varieties should parallel that of any phonological system, none of which are homogeneous. A phonological description of Educated British English (EBE), he advises would start with describing "the phonological systems of a large number of speakers of EBE . . . Characterization of the phonology of EBE then is the characterization of the *invariance and variability of the phonological systems of individual speakers of EBE*" (italics original in Mohanan 1992: 126). The same approach, he argues, applies when describing any phonological system.

In this Element, I aim to characterize uniformity and variability in IndE accents by looking for features that are shared or systematically vary across the speech of Indian users of English. If a shared set of characteristics belonging to accents that are IndE exists, then the next question is where to look for them. In the research reviewed in the following, including my own, a common population for investigating both a standard and variations has been students, especially at urban English-medium universities. As students are available, cheap, and numerous, this is obviously a sample of convenience to academic researchers, but it also bears other advantages in the search for commonalities across IndE. The majority of users of IndE are urban, so this population is representative in that way. Relatively young speakers, generally twenty to thirty years old, are not as likely to have spent extensive time outside of India, so their linguistic background has been influenced by fewer complicating factors. Furthermore, to be proficient by that age makes it more likely that they began their acquisition of English early; earlier acquisition means less L1 influence (e.g., Flege et al. 1995). This group also may have the advantage of reflecting the more contemporaneous pedagogical approaches, for example, involving teachers and linguistic models from within India, and younger speakers, or at least young women, are expected to show where language change is heading. Collecting their speech in a laboratory and by recording tasks such as reading should prompt them to use their most acrolectal variety as the most appropriate for the situation. So if we suspect that acrolectal versions are the most likely to share characteristics across regions or the entire nation, then we should be studying the speech of urban, highly-educated, regular users of English, who started learning early. As for the disadvantages of relying on this group, they are not representative of a large part of India, or even of English-using India. For the acrolectal speakers who they might represent, such young speakers have not had as much time to develop the patterns of use typical of more mature users of English, and they may not have reached their fullest proficiency, ease of use, or ability to manipulate features sociolinguistically. Limited travel and other experience may also have limited their awareness of accent features as identity markers. Whatever findings we build up from current research will need to be supplemented with studies of speakers from a wider range of ages, communities, and contexts.

How can we know when we have an IndE feature of the intended sort, whether the epitome of a homogeneous standard or a member of a set of standards (regional, social, etc.) distinct from learners errors? Fortunately, there are ways to distinguish stabilized features that belong to varieties from features that arise when speakers are still learning or have fossilized errors. These factors include stability, patterned (non-random) use, and evaluation as a norm within a speech community, whether as determined by linguistic behavior or explicitly sanctioned by authorities like teachers or textbooks (Bamgbose 1998, Sharma 2005, van Rooy 2011). Sharma (2005) provides an example from IndE when she investigates both phonological and grammatical features in the speech of twelve Indian speakers of English living in the USA. For many of the grammatical features, increased use of a nonstandard feature correlates with lower proficiency, suggesting that L2 learning is still in progress, while for the use of articles and for the phonological features, there is no such correlation; features that relate to IndE phonology are "spread more evenly and broadly across speakers" (2005: 202). Although not all studies provide enough data to test for a correlation, comparing across studies can also provide support for features as varietal rather than reflecting incomplete learning.

2.4 Sources of Uniformity and Variability

In addition to describing accent characteristics reflecting uniformity and variability within IndE, I will look for explanations for their presence. Here I provide a brief introduction to the different kinds of sources, each of which has been argued to introduce uniformity, variability, or potentially both into IndE accent(s). English in India, like English in Great Britain itself, has developed in a context of languages and language varieties in contact. Theories of language development under these circumstances (e.g., Mufwene 2001, Schneider 2003, 2007, Trudgill 2004) invoke the effects of founder varieties, multiple norms, substrates, and linguistic universals, along with the processes of koineization (dialect unification). As IndE is currently transmitted primarily through school, the educational system may also play a role.

The first factor to consider is the characteristics of the English(es) that were brought to India during the early development of IndE. The contribution of early varieties may have had an outsized impact, as it has been observed that structural features in languages/varieties shaped extensively by colonialism and contact "have been predetermined to a large extent (though not exclusively!) by characteristics of the vernaculars spoken by the populations that founded the colonies in which they developed" (Mufwene 2001: 28–29). To evaluate founder effects on IndE means examining the forms of English brought to and used in India in previous centuries, and the British who brought English first to India were not monolithic in their accents. Mufwene notes that "English in the British Isles was undergoing changes during the colonization of the Americas, Africa, and Asia by Western European nations. Since English was never regionally homogeneous before the seventeenth century, the metropolitan population reshuffling was producing various new local and regional varieties" (2001: 158). Furthermore, although some British officials may have spoken an early form of a Southern Standard English variety, most new arrivals were not speakers of the socially most desirable varieties. Krishnaswamy and Burde (1998) observe that in the first phase (1600–1757), "those who came to India were mostly uneducated merchants, sailors, and soldiers" (1998: 80), along with missionaries who probably had some education, though likely in Latin rather than English. Mesthrie and Bhatt (2008: 192) argue that sailor varieties "must have drawn on non-standard English, English regional dialects, and English slang," while Mehrotra (1998: 5) asserts that "in the formative period 'Northern British dialects and Cockney' constituted the major English language influences in India" (quoted in Schneider 2007: 163). Thus, the varieties of English present during the earliest stages of IndE formation included a range of dialects and sociolects from within England.

Further afield, the Scottish, Welsh, and Irish also arrived early in India and potentially influenced the early formation of IndE. McGilvary (2011) details evidence that Scottish soldiers, merchants, civil servants, etc., had reached India during the formative years of English spread, beginning around 1725, and estimates some 3,500–4,000 Scots went to India during the following century, forming one of the largest European presences after the English. Nihalani et al. (1979) also report that "Surveys made so far have revealed what is believed to be Scottish or Welsh influence in the English spoken by Indians in certain parts of the country, and these influences have been attributed to the Scots and Welsh teachers who worked in these regions" (1979: 204). Finally, Bernaisch and Koch (2016) argue that AmE should not be overlooked either, both because of its current presence in the form of US media, "but also because a number of native speakers of AmE started their work as missionaries in India from the beginning of the 19th century onwards" (2016: 120). American missionaries were particularly active in the northeast, establishing schools as well as missions from the 1830s, contemporaneously with British expansion into the area (Barpujari 1986). While BrE speakers in India greatly outnumbered AmE speakers, nonetheless the presence of AmE speakers means their features were available in the language ecology of India at an early stage. Having diverse sources of accent features in the pool from the beginning can contribute to a diversity of accent features in IndE today; on the other hand, founder varieties may lead to uniformity, as argued in Domange (2011, 2015), who investigates a vowel contrast in IndE that may have survived from early in the contact period and still persists widely (see Section 4.2.3).

Mufwene (2001) uses the general principles of evolution to understand the development of individual language varieties, treating language as a species in the context of a linguistic ecology, with individual speakers as "agents of language evolution" (2001: 149). With a variety of English dialects combined with local languages and multilingualism, IndE arose in an environment where speakers had multiple options available in their linguistic ecology.

Ansaldo (2009) describes the selection and replication of some features over others as influenced by factors like the social value associated with options or the frequency of exposure to an option. Multiple sources providing the same option, making it more densely represented among the pool of choices, favors selection and replication, potentially leading to change as in other evolving systems. Futhermore, "[m]ore often than not, identical and innovative replication are combined in contact ecologies, as contact language formation often arises out of the tension between, on the one hand, the convergence to external linguistic norms, and, on the other, the preservation of a degree of linguistic differentiation for the purpose of in-group identification" (Ansaldo 2009: 136).

Speakers of IndE come from a variety of backgrounds and geographic locations, potentially leading to such differentiation of different local norms, but as the primary use of English in India is communication with other English users in India, contact among speakers of different varieties of IndE may also play a role. Dialect contact requires accommodation for successful communication, and potentially leads to dialect leveling or the formation of a koiné, which Mesthrie and Bhatt (2008: 179) define as "a variety essentially arising out of contact involving dialects of the same language." With urbanization growing in India over the last fifty years, koineization may emerge especially in urban contexts where speakers come together from different states, regions, and L1s, and therefore possibly different IndEs; accommodation in the urban contact situation may lead to a koineization with a deregionalizing effect (Kohli 2017), and hence more uniformity across IndE varieties.

The fact that most users of English in India are multilingual, having acquired (or started acquiring) another language before English, is often treated as the major contributor to the linguistic characteristics of IndE, whether historically or synchronically (e.g., Kachru 1983, Sirsa & Redford 2013, Sharma 2017). Second language acquisition (SLA) theory suggests two general factors that may influence the phonetic and phonological characteristics of speakers of multiple languages: transfer and markedness. Transfer means that features of a language acquired earlier are carried into languages acquired later, and in the context of India, this may promote both uniformity and variability. As mentioned, Indo-Aryan and Dravidian languages long in contact have come to share phonetic and phonological features, such as retroflexion; if common features are transferred into IndE, they can be a source of uniformity. On the other hand, the languages of India diverge in numerous ways, such as the number and type of vowel and consonant contrasts, and transfer of these characteristics can lead to diversity. Transfer need not be attributed to the current learners and speakers of IndE, especially English-medium speakers exposed to English early enough to acquire a target language without accent (Flege 1991, Flege et al. 1995). Sirsa and Redford (2013) favor the hypothesis that there is a common IndE target separate from Indian L1s, but observe that this "does not contradict the idea that IE phonology reflects indigenous Indian languages influences; it merely suggests that these influences are historical in nature" (2013: 394–395).

A second factor arising in SLA that may have shaped IndE, whether historically or synchronically, is the role of markedness or universals, which promote uniformity when less marked forms are adopted, following language universals. SLA research suggests learners may follow some patterns of acquisition regardless of the structure of their first languages, for example, producing voiceless obstruents in coda positions before voiced (e.g., Broselow et al. 1998). Markedness has also been invoked in studies of contact-induced language change, including the development of vernacular varieties of English and New Englishes (e.g., Filppula et al. 2009, Mukherjee & Hundt 2011, Wiltshire 2014). Trudgill (2004: 119–120) argues that markedness can be a determining factor in dialect leveling as well, as "the reduction of variants over time is thus not haphazard from the point of view of purely linguistic forces, either: degree of linguistic markedness may be involved, such that the unmarked forms may have the edge in the competition for survival." The complex interactions of feature competition, however, may produce new patterns that do not follow markedness principles; Mohanan and Mohanan (2003) discuss Malayalee English as an example of a variety developing a pattern that matches neither Malayalam nor any founder source, resulting in a more complex and marked system.

Education is another factor that can prove unifying or dividing. Insofar as teachers within India spread the same norms, the educational system is unifying. An emphasis on written rather than spoken English can lead to orthography as a factor as well. Nagarajan (1985), for example, notes that gemmination is common in words spelled with double consonants (e.g. *butter*, *fully*), while the lack of aspiration in stops spelled <p, t, k> has also been attributed to orthography (e.g., Shuja 1995, Sailaja 2009). Education can be a source of divergence as well, as providers of English-medium education may draw on different norms, most notably in the convent education system where, as Sharma (2017) notes, features of Anglo-Indian varieties (Coelho 1997) may be transmitted, thus disseminating the contrasts and phonetics of specific dialects.

The issue of whether the accents of Indian speakers of English, or features of these accents, tend to be monolithic or heterogeneous can be examined from an external evaluation of acoustic characteristics of speech or an internal evaluation of perception in two senses: ability to perceive differences among speakers of different varieties and perceptions about internal variation within IndE. A great deal of research has examined the acoustic characteristics of consonants, vowels, and suprasegmentals in the English of speakers from India, and I primarily draw on this to find features that are likely candidates for uniformity or variability; I also provide some additional analyses from my own data to verify claims about the distribution of features in Sections 3.2.2 and 4.2.3. Unless otherwise specified, the research cited here draws on a population that is young (in their twenties to early thirties), educated (past college graduation), and urban. Furthermore, in order to illustrate the characteristics discussed in the following, I provide spectrograms and sound samples from five speakers from this population. As Delhi-Hindi speakers are already well-represented in the literature, I have diversified to a range of cities-L1s: Chennai-Tamil, Mumbai-Marathi, Mysore-Kannada, Shillong-Khasi, Tinsukia-Assamese (see Appendix for more detail); apart from the Shillong-Khasi speaker, who was recorded in 2013, the other recordings were made in 2020 solely for the purposes of illustration rather than analysis.

The next three sections focus on results from the external perspective by looking at what has been discovered for consonants (Section 3), vowels (Section 4), and suprasegmentals (Section 5). In each, I examine characteristics of the accents of IndE, and where possible, investigate sources of these features in founder varieties, koineization, second language effects, and education.

3 Consonants

Differences among segments can be described as systematic (the number/type of contrasts), realizational (the actual pronunciations of phonemes), or distributional (restrictions on occurrence) (Wells 1982). I focus on the first two aspects here, especially the realizational differences which acoustics can evaluate, although these results also shed light on contrasts. Descriptions of a "standard" IndE system tend to share a great deal in common, and descriptions of varieties are often framed in terms of divergence from those standards. Hence I will present a standard description (Section 3.1) and then discuss some major

characteristics which may either be shared across IndE varieties or be a source
of distinction among them, discussing acoustic research and likely sources of
these characteristics (Section 3.2). Finally, I will provide an overview of
commonalities and differences documented thus far (Section 3.3).

3.1 Standard Descriptions of the IndE Consonant System

A system of General Indian English (GIE) was proposed in the 1970s as an
educational model for use in India (CIEFL 1972, Bansal & Harrison 2013
[1972]), and the consonants of this model are given in Table 2. Symbols in
parentheses designate alternative pronunciations that are considered acceptable.

Pandey (2015: 303) writes that "in spite of some regional variation in its
pronunciation, there is considerable stability in GIE to bear a description," and
most of this model has not changed in later descriptions. Minor changes have
been proposed; for example, Bansal (1983) does not list any stops with aspiration apart from the voiceless dental stop, while Pandey (2015) adds voiced
aspirated stops [bʱ dʱ gʱ] used as spelling pronunciations for <*bh, dh, gh*>.
Further differences between Table 2 and later proposals will be discussed as
they arise in the following with respect to the characteristics being examined.

3.2 Potential Consonantal Characteristics of IndE Varieties

Numerous aspects of this system have been researched, as either differing
internally within IndE varieties or as collectively distinguishing IndE varieties
from other major varieties of English. For example, the system has dental and
retroflex stops, but no dental fricatives or alveolar stops, the contrast between
homorganic stops may or may not involve aspiration, two labial approximants
are listed (ʋ/w), and the rhotic is symbolized as [r] but written in the approximant row. Ideally, every aspect of the consonant system should be evaluated, as
we do not know whether other differences are currently overlooked. Mohanan
(1992) argues that an analysis based on describing a variety on its own terms
may reveal systematicity that cannot be discovered by descriptions that compare a variety to some external norm, and he illustrates with an alveolar-
retroflex distinction uniquely made in Malayalee English (Mohanan &
Mohanan 2003). It is likely that further variety-internal research will illuminate
further phonetic and phonological aspects of IndE systems. For the present
Element, however, I focus on what we currently know about the already
observed characteristics, and within that set, on the abovementioned features:
places of articulation, voicing/aspiration, labial approximants, and rhotics.
Throughout, I rely on studies that specify that their speakers are educated
young users of English who started learning early and attended English-

Table 2 CIEFL's consonant inventory of GIE (CIEFL 1972: 3)

	Labial	Labio-dental	Dental	Alveolar	Post-alveolar	Retroflex	Palatal	Velar	Glottal
Stop	p(pʰ) b		(t̪)t̪ʰ d̪			ʈ(ʈʰ) ɖ		k(kʰ) g	
Affricate					ʧ(ʧʰ) ʤ				
Nasal	m			n				ŋ	
Fricative		f		s z	ʃ				h
Approx	ʋ/w			r			j		
LatAppr				l		(ɭ)			

medium schools, and I will mention if a study specifies a different set of speakers.

3.2.1 Stop Places of Articulation

IndE contrasts labial and velar stops, like other Englishes, and is generally said to have stops at two further places of articulation: retroflex and dental. Retroflexes have attracted attention not only because their use in IndE distinguishes it from other Englishes, but also because there is variation within IndE. Dental stops, said to be the common IndE pronunciation of the <*th*> spelling, are found widely in other varieties of English but exploration of the extent and limits of their use in IndE has only just begun.

Retroflexes

Most models, like Table 2, list retroflexes, and most descriptions of IndE mention the use of retroflex stops or inconsistent variation between retroflexes and alveolars (Kachru 1983, Nair 1996). Sahgal and Agnihotri (1988) describe their middle-class speakers as more often using alveolars instead of retroflexes, although they did not measure their tokens acoustically. Retroflexion can be quantified using the difference between F3 and F2 at vowel offset, and this metric has been used to evaluate retroflexes in the IndE of speakers of Dravidian and Indo-Aryan languages. Wiltshire and Harnsberger (2006) compared the IndE of L1 Tamil[3] and Gujarati speakers, finding that all speakers used retroflex stops; furthermore, their F2 and F3 transitions showed no significant difference in degree of retroflexion between the rather small (five each) speaker groups. We suggested that this characteristic should be studied in other groups, since degree of retroflexion differs across the languages of India, such as Hindi, Telugu, and Tamil (Ladefoged & Bhaskararao 1983); similar retroflexion across IndE may indicate convergence toward an IndE norm. Sirsa and Redford (2013) compared the English of L1 Telugu and Hindi speakers (seven each), and, furthermore, checked retroflexion within the L1s of these same speakers. While the L1s did differ, particularly in terms of which consonant (/ʈ/ or /ɖ/) was produced with more retroflexion, the degree of retroflexion in IndE did not differ between the two groups. Sirsa & Redford concluded that "native language differences were evident, but IE targets were constant across speakers with different language backgrounds" (2013: 400).

Figure 2 provides a spectrogram of retroflex stops initially and finally by the Chennai-Tamil speaker and intervocalically by the Mumbai-Marathi

---

[3] Two Tamil speakers in this study did not attend English-medium schools and began learning English as a subject at ages 8 and 14.

Figure 2 Retroflex stops in "toy", "foot" (Chennai-Tamil), "letter" (Mumbai-Marathi).

Sound 2 Audio file available at www.cambridge.org/wiltshire

speaker, with formants circled to show the F2 and F3 transitions. Throughout this Element, the sounds used in the figures can be heard via the link in the caption.

In the two studies mentioned thus far, one Southern-Dravidian (Tamil, Telugu) and one Northern-Indo-Aryan (Gujarati, Hindi) L1 group were compared, and the degree of retroflexion in their IndE was comparable. However, Wiltshire (2005) found that speakers from northeast India lack retroflexes and use alveolars and dentals instead, based on recordings by speakers of three Tibeto-Burman languages (Angami, Ao, and Mizo).[4] Speakers of other L1s from the northeast also generally lack retroflexes, as shown in Figure 3, with alveolars initially and finally from the Tinsukia-Assamese speaker, and intervocalically from the Shillong-Khasi speaker. Unlike Figure 2, the F2 and F3 do not converge. With the northeast varieties lacking retroflex stops, IndE is not uniform on this characteristic; however, for those speakers who do use retroflexes, evidence suggests that IndE provides the norms rather than their L1s.

Transfer, historic and current, supports both the uniformity and variability. Retroflexes are common in Dravidian and Indo-Aryan languages (Masica 1991, Krishnamurti 2003), and absent in Austroasiatic languages such as Khasi (Sharma 2014) and in the Tibeto-Burman languages whose English is studied in Wiltshire (2005). As observed there, it is unclear whether the transfer should be considered positive or negative. Early IndE learners in the northeast may have been taught by speakers of British or American varieties, who lacked retroflex stops, but many of my subjects reported being taught by IndE speakers from elsewhere in India, who likely did use retroflexes, so they are resisting the more general IndE model by continuing to use alveolars and dentals.

---

[4] One Mizo speaker in the study began English as a subject at age twelve; all others attended English-medium schools from age four or five.

Figure 3 Alveolar stops in "toy", "foot" (Tinsukia-Assamese), "betting" (Shillong-Khasi).

Sound 3 Audio file available at www.cambridge.org/wiltshire

Dental Stops

The spelling <*th*> is pronounced in a variety of ways in English dialects and sociolects around the world, including as dental fricatives (Standard RP, AmE), dental stops (parts of NY, Ireland), and labiodental fricatives (sociolects in London, AAVE). Within India, standard descriptions suggest stop pronunciations: voiceless aspirated dental stop [t̪ʰ] in words like *thought*, and voiced unaspirated dental stop [d̪] in words like *though* (CIEFL 1972, Gargesh 2004, Pandey 2015). Such pronunciations have been noted widely in descriptive works, including in Tamil English (Nagarajan 1985), Western Uttar Pradesh Hindi/Urdu English (Shuja 1995), and Tibeto-Burman IndE (Wiltshire 2005).

However, Sailaja (2009) observes that interdental fricative pronunciations do occur in IndE, at least voiceless [θ], though voiced "[ð] is almost completely missing" (Sailaja 2009: 21). Domange (2011) investigates the extent to which this holds true for a group of ten male speakers in South Delhi. Domange finds that although overall dental fricative use is rare, about 13 per cent of total tokens, yet "there is no speaker who does not produce these fricatives" (2011: 29). He also finds that fricative realizations are sensitive to linguistic context (e.g., more likely after sonorants and vowels), and overall, the voiceless dental fricative is more likely than the voiced, as Sailaja (2009) claimed. Furthermore, speakers who reported using English more used dental fricatives more. When Domange focused on the pattern among higher use speakers only, there was also a numerical tendency toward using more fricatives in the more formal styles, suggesting that "only the group of speakers using the English language the most takes advantage of its sociolinguistic potential" (Domange 2011: 33).

Figure 4a shows the dental stops initially, finally, and intervocalically, used by the Mumbai-Marathi, Mysore-Kannada, and Tinsukia-Assamese speakers. When voiceless, the dental stop is also aspirated. Figure 4b, on the other hand, provides examples from the Shillong-Khasi speaker who tends to use fricatives,

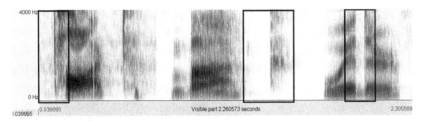

Figure 4a Dental stops in "thought" (Mumbai-Marathi), "bath" (Mysore-Kannada), "weather" (Tinsukia-Assamese).

Sound 4a Audio file available at www.cambridge.org/wiltshire

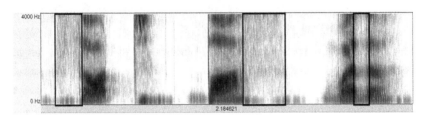

Figure 4b Dental fricatives in "thought", "bath", "weather" (Shillong-Khasi).

Sound 4b Audio file available at www.cambridge.org/wiltshire

especially in this formal data collection situation; his fricatives are highlighted and occur here in initial, final, and intervocalic position. Thus, while the use of dental stops in IndE is widespread, it is not uniform; the extent and conditioning of fricative use bears more investigation.

The source of dental stop usage can be transfer or markedness, whether in historical acquisition or current transmission or both. Most, if not all, Indian languages have dental stops. Dental fricatives are absent from most languages of India and the world (Maddieson 1984), indicating that they are marked sounds, while Lombardi (2003) notes that the replacement of dental fricatives with dental stops, preserving place, is the least marked and most widespread option in second language acquisition. There may also be founder effects, as dental stops are used in Irish English (Hickey 1986), a contributor to the early feature pool.

Orthography is often cited as a source of the pronunciation, especially for learners literate in an L1 which distinguishes aspirated and unaspirated stops both phonetically and orthographically. Sailaja proposes spelling is responsible for the voiceless aspirated dental stop: "Since most of the words in which this sound is expected are written with<*th*>, aspiration of the plosive is heard"

(Sailaja 2009: 21). However, this does not explain the lack of aspiration on voiced dental stops, despite the existence of /d̪ʰ/ in many Indian languages. Barron (1961) rejected the spelling pronunciation explanation alone, noting that the spelling <t> for many speakers corresponds with a retroflex stop in IndE, so a spelling-based explanation should therefore predict <th> to correspond to an aspirated retroflex stop. Foreshadowing Lombardi (2003), Barron proposes instead that preservation of dental place is more important to Indian listeners and speakers than preservation of manner:

> It seems clear, therefore, that from the earliest days of the English language in India, /θ/ and /ð/ have been heard and accepted as dental plosives and not as fricatives. It is their dentality that has made the impression on the Indian ear and they have been accepted as plosives because the Indian languages have only plosives in that position. (Barron 1961: 85)

The presence of dental stops in the pool, from Indian substrates and English, along with their lack of markedness, conspired to make them widespread in IndE, while external varieties perhaps provide the fricative option for use as a sociolinguistic marker of formality.

3.2.2 Voice/Voiceless Contrast

Like other Englishes, IndE makes a two-way contrast between stops at each place of articulation (p vs. b, k vs. g, etc.), called "voiced" and "voiceless." The voiceless stops have been widely described as tending to lack aspiration or to vary "unsystematically" between aspirated and unaspirated in IndE (CIEFL 1972, Bansal & Harrison 2013 [1972], Pandey 2015), while the realization of voiced stops as prevoiced is also occasionally noted (Davis & Beckman 1983, Wiltshire & Harnsberger 2006). In terms of the phonetics of the contrast, the realizations of both types of stop suggest a feature that widely, possibly uniformly, characterizes IndE varieties across India.

Phonetically, this contrast can be measured in terms of Voice Onset Time (VOT), operationalized by Lisker & Abramson (1964: 389) as the "interval between the release of the stop and the onset of glottal vibration." VOT provides three categories cross-linguistically for contrasting homorganic stops: "voiced," where voicing precedes the stop release resulting in a negative VOT; "voiceless unaspirated," where voicing follows quickly after the release so that the VOT is positive and small; and "voiceless aspirated," where voicing does not begin until well after the stop release so that the VOT is positive and large. The two-way contrast in IndE involves phonetically voiced vs. voiceless unaspirated or aspirated stops, and this appears to be true regardless of the L1 or region of the speakers (Davis & Beckman 1983, Shuja 1995, Nair 1996, Coelho 1997, Wiltshire & Harnsberger 2006; Awan & Stine 2011, Sirsa & Redford 2013, McCullough 2013).

Davis and Beckman (1983) examined the contrast in IndE vs. AmE speakers and found that Indian speakers generally prevoiced their voiced stops, while voiceless stops had short lag times. Their five speakers all had Hindi as their L1 but were living in the USA, four for over three years and one for only six months. This last IndE speaker had even longer lead times for the voiced and less voicing lag for the voiceless tokens, suggesting experience with AmE had affected the other speakers. Wiltshire and Harnsberger (2006), using subjects in India, found that both Tamil and Gujarati L1 speakers consistently distinguished between voiced and voiceless stops in their English, with the voiced /b/ showing long negative VOTs averaging –86 and –97 ms for Gujarati and Tamil groups respectively. McCullough (2013) examined acoustic properties that might be responsible for foreign accent perceptions in English, including VOT. Among her L1 Hindi speakers, she determined that a substantial portion of their voiced tokens were prevoiced, unlike the productions by speakers from other L1 backgrounds (McCullough 2013: 56). For the voiceless stops, Awan & Stine (2011) found that their twenty IndE speakers from eight L1 backgrounds had significantly shorter VOT times than those of twenty AmE speakers, while Sirsa and Redford (2013) compared IndE speakers from Hindi and Telugu L1 groups and established that the short lag VOT of their voiceless stops in English did not differ significantly between the two (2013: 400), suggesting a common target among educated IndE speakers.

I have examined the voicing contrast in speakers from a variety of L1s using my own data gathered in India in 2003, 2013, and 2019. The 2003 data consists of five speakers each of different L1s, recorded in Hyderabad, and the data used here includes speakers of eleven L1s (Angami, Ao, Bengali, Gujarati, Hindi, Kannada, Malayalam, Mizo, Oriya, Tamil, and Telugu). The 2013 and 2019 data were collected in Guwahati, Assam, in collaboration with Professor Priyankoo Sarmah of IIT-Guwahati; in 2013, we recorded five speakers each with L1s Bodo, Meitei, and Khasi, while the 2019 study recorded twenty L1 speakers of Assamese. In all three instances, the IndE speakers were in their twenties to early thirties, highly educated, and living in urban environments. They were recorded reading word lists, sentences, and paragraphs, and being interviewed about their language background; the VOT measures here are based on the word lists only.

From the 2019 data, Priyankoo Sarmah and I have measured the VOT of word-initial voiced and voiceless English stops (ten tokens of each: [b d g p t k]) produced by a subset of L1 Assamese speakers. I have also measured the VOT of initial [b] in fifteen words produced by each speaker of the diverse set of fourteen Indian L1s from the 2003 and 2013 data. The results support the analysis of IndE as distinguishing prevoiced stops from voiceless. Among the Assamese speakers of IndE, voiceless stops are generally unaspirated (n = 3 speakers, mean VOTs [p]: 13 ms, [t]: 15 ms, [k]: 26 ms), while voiced stops are generally prevoiced (n = 4, means [b]: -85 ms, [d]: -103 ms, [g]: -87 ms). The [b] s measured were also prevoiced within each of the 14 L1 groups and overall (n = 70, mean [b]: -86 ms). Heavily prevoiced stops in word-initial position may thus be a characteristic of IndE more generally.

To illustrate the prevoicing, Figure 5 provides spectrograms of initial voiced stops produced by the Tinsukia-Assamese, Mysore-Kannada, and Chennai-Tamil speakers, with prevoicing indicated in a box. On some utterances, the prevoicing is also prenasalized.

McCullough's (2013) study not only found a difference between the VOTs of her AmE and IndE speakers, but also found that this was one of the most important cues in triggering AmE listeners to recognize the speech as IndE. The realization of the contrast may contribute to the recognition of an IndE accent because it differs from typical AmE and BrE varieties, in which word-initial voiceless stops in isolation tend to be not only voiceless but also aspirated, while voiced stops show a bimodal distribution even within the same variety of English, being realized as prevoiced or voiceless unaspirated (Docherty 1992, Chodroff & Wilson 2017). For many speakers, the norm is to produce /b d g/ with phonetically voiceless unaspirated stops, thus contrasting unaspirated with aspirated stops. This results in the phonetic sounds [p t k] word-initially playing the role of the "voiced" stops in AmE and BrE, while identical sounds are the "voiceless" member of the contrast for IndE speakers, raising the potential for misperception. Davis and Beckman (1983) documented this in a perception experiment with tokens from their five IndE and five AmE

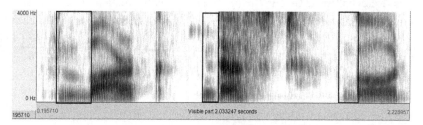

Figure 5 Prevoicing in "bark" (Tinsukia-Assamese), "dust" (Mysore-Kannada), "goat" (Chennai-Tamil)

Sound 5 Audio file available at www.cambridge.org/wiltshire

speakers played back to all ten for identification of the word-initial sound as /p
t k b d g/. They found that the AmE speakers misidentified IndE voiceless /p t k/
nearly 30 per cent of the time, particularly mislabeling tokens by the speaker
most recently from India, while the IndE listeners, on the other hand, had the
most difficulty identifying the /b d g/ of AmE speakers, particularly one AmE
speaker who consistently produced these with short lag.

Because of the phonetics of their contrast, AmE and BrE varieties are
described as "aspirating" languages, like many other Germanic languages. By
contrast, IndE seems to belong to the set of "voicing" languages, such as
Russian and Spanish (see Beckman et al. 2013 and references therein).
Following from the distinction are predictions, including that sonorant consonants after voiceless stops in onset clusters should be fully voiced in voicing
languages, unlike in AmE and BrE, which devoice them (Iverson & Salmons
1995). In the Assamese speakers of English mentioned above, I examined the
voicing of glides in word-initial /pr, pl, tr, kr, kl/ clusters in twelve words each
for five speakers, and found the approximants fully voiced, supporting the claim
that IndE uses voice rather than aspiration to distinguish its stops.

Figure 6 shows a spectrogram of an IndE (on the left) and an AmE (right)
production of the word "plant." The boxes indicates the release of the /p/ and the
following /l/, showing the lateral clearly voiced for the IndE speaker and most of
the lateral voiceless for the AmE speaker.

The use of [voice] for the contrast is not likely due to transfer alone. Although
[voice] is certainly used in many Indian languages, there is a diversity of
laryngeal contrasts in voicing and aspiration as shown in Table 3 for the
languages measured for [b], as discussed. The contrast of prevoiced vs. voiceless stops appears to be used in IndE regardless of the number or type of voice/
aspiration contrasts in the L1 of the speaker.

Furthermore, although the VOT of L2 English speakers can vary depending
on age of acquisition, Flege (1991) showed that the VOTs of bilinguals who

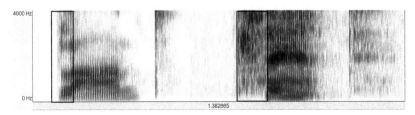

Figure 6 No approximant devoicing in IndE (Tinsukia-Assamese) vs. devoicing
in AmE "plant."

Sound 6 Audio file available at www.cambridge.org/wiltshire

Table 3 Number/type of contrasts in the oral stops of L1s used for voicing measurements

# of contrasts	Features of contrast	Languages
1	[]	Tamil (e.g., /p/ with allophonic [b] in native words)
2	[voice]	Bodo (e.g., /p b/)
2	[spr glot]	Ao, Meitei (e.g., /pʰ p/)
3	[spr glot], [voice]	Angami, Mizo (e.g., /pʰ p b/)
4	[spr glot], [voice]	Assamese, Bengali, Gujarati, Kannada, Khasi, Hindi, Malayalam, Oriya, Telugu (e.g., /pʰ p b bʱ/)

began "early" (age five to six) did not differ from those of English monolinguals. This supports the claim that early learners should be able to establish appropriate phonetic targets in an L2, so that the VOTs of these early learners indicates an IndE target rather than transfer from L1s.

If we try to explain the origins of the IndE norms using cross-linguistic markedness, we would need to argue that voiceless unaspirated stops were less marked than aspirated ones or the contrast of voicing less marked than that of aspiration. However, Vaux & Samuels (2005) argue that voiceless aspirated stops are less marked than unaspirated, and that the contrast of aspirated–unaspirated stop is less marked than that of voiced–voiceless unaspirated. This would make the BrE/AmE system less marked than the IndE system. Furthermore, a markedness explanation would suggest that voiced–voiceless systems should be acquired earlier than unaspirated–aspirated, while evidence suggests that the acquisition of aspirated voiceless stops precedes that of prevoiced stops (Davis 1995). If true, this means that speakers of IndE are neither transferring not defaulting to an unmarked system.

Dialects and varieties of English differ in how the contrast is realized (Scobbie 2006, Jacewicz et al. 2009, Shahidi & Aman 2011), and a potential source of explanation for the IndE system lies in founder effects. Scottish English has been observed to have voiceless stops with little aspiration and voiced stops with prevoicing, though it may now be undergoing change toward higher VOTs (Scobbie 2006, Stuart-Smith et al. 2015, Sonderegger et al. 2020). Thus, the use of [voice] to contrast stops was available in the feature pool during the establishment of founder varieties, from at least one British variety and from many local Indian languages.

Another factor may be orthography for those Indian languages that contrast voiced-voiceless and unaspirated-aspirated. Because the writing systems of such languages distinguish aspirated and unaspirated sounds, learners of a new system who see an orthographically unadorned voiceless stop such as <p> would assume it is meant to convey the unaspirated phoneme /p/ rather than /pʰ/ (Shuja 1995, Wiltshire & Harnsberger 2006). Similarly, in languages with prevoiced sounds, an association between the orthographic /b/ in the L1 and the English may support prevoicing. Such an explanation does not help synchronically with a language like Tamil, which has no voiced/voiceless distinction in the orthography, suggesting that current IndE speakers from such backgrounds must have adopted an IndE norm. Furthermore, the education system may reinforce IndE norms. My colleague Priyankoo Sarmah recalls that during his schooling in the 1990s, he and other students who had listened to CNN or the BBC tried using aspiration on voiceless stops, but remembers "being told off a couple of times, because I tried to pronounce English 'like a sahib'" (personal communication 1/16/20).

3.2.3 Labiodental Fricatives and Labiodental/Labiovelar Approximants: v/ʊ/w

While English orthography includes a contrast between the spellings <v> and <w>, many descriptions claim that IndE speakers do not make a contrast between them. CIEFL (1972) lists the labiodental and labiovelar approximants, [ʊ] and [w], as allophonic variations of each other with no labiodental fricative [v] in the system, while Bansal lists the phoneme as /v/ as in "vain, wait" but gives its phonetics as labiodental approximant [ʊ] or weakly rounded [w] (Bansal 1976: 18). Pandey (2015) lists only the labiodental approximant, which he says is used for both <w> and <v>. Sailaja (2009), on the other hand, says that only nonstandard varieties merge the contrast, while Standard IndE preserves it as the labiovelar approximant [w] vs. either the labiodental approximant [ʊ] or a labiodental fricative with less frication than British [v].

More detailed research supports Sailaja's claim that reports of a complete absence of contrast are premature. Realizations of <v>, <w> and the contrast may be variable both across India and within communities of IndE speakers. Sahgal and Agnihotri (1988) report a widespread use of [ʊ] and more limited use of [w] (20–33 per cent of the time) for their speakers in Delhi, while Chand (2009), also based in Delhi, found that "No speaker completely merges the two phonemes, and speakers are variable in how frequently they pronounce [w] for /v/" (2009: 415). Wiltshire and Harnsberger (2006) described Gujarati L1 speakers as showing free variation between the labiodental and labiovelar approximants, with [ʊ] more frequent, while most Tamil L1 speakers also used [ʋ] for both <v> and <w> spellings, but all used [w] for at least some of the words spelled with <w>. One Tamil speaker used [w] for all words spelled with <w> and used [v]/[ʋ] for those with <v>, a pattern Wiltshire (2015) found repeated in other Dravidian L1 (Malayalam, Telugu, Kannada) speakers. Similarly, Wiltshire (2005) found that Tibeto-Burman L1 speakers of English can and do produce the labiodental fricative, and also "seem to keep a distinction, using [w] for most words spelled with a <w>, and [v]/[ʋ] for words spelled with a <v> " (2005: 284). Perhaps Dravidian and Tibeto-Burman speakers have developed their own patterns in IndE, distinct from Indo-Aryan speakers.

The aforementioned studies generally involved judgments by the researchers, sometimes supported by spectrograms, as to the nature of the phonetic sounds reported. In the most detailed acoustic study, Fuchs (2019) examines the speech of twenty IndE speakers from four L1 backgrounds: Hindi, Bengali, Telugu, and Malayalam.[5] Fuchs measured three acoustic characteristics, and reported results for orthographic <v/w> in onset position. For spectral centroid, an indicator of frication, he found no difference between <v>/<w> sounds produced by the IndE group and no differences within the groups based on L1, indicating that the IndE speakers uniformly were not producing a fricative or distinguishing orthographic <v>/<w> by frication. For the second formant measure, which indicates lip rounding and velar constriction when low, IndE speakers do make a distinction: <v> is produced with a significantly higher F2 than <w>, indicating that the labiodental has less lip rounding and velar constriction. Though there were numerical differences between L1 groups, those were not statistically significant. For F3, which indicates lip rounding (and not velar constriction), Fuchs again finds a significant difference between <v>/<w> in IndE, but only after vowels. The results overall indicate that the contrast is between two approximants, one with more lip rounding and velar constriction ([w]) than the other ([ʋ]), and that the L1 groups did not differ on these measures. Comparing the IndE tokens with those of ten speakers of BrE, Fuchs also found that the magnitude of the differences between the two sounds were smaller for IndE speakers (Fuchs 2019: 1385), and noted that the perceptibility of the differences remains untested. Fuchs suggests that the contrast is in a state of "near-merger," converging on an approximant with some rounding and velar raising for both <v>/<w>, though the study provides no evidence of direction of change. His results do show, however, that phonetic differences distinguish

---

[5] All except one were English-medium educated.

between the two sounds, with no differences across these L1 groups in current IndE.

Figure 7 provides a minimal pair ("vest" "west") produced by the Chennai-Tamil speaker, where the initial sound in "vest" has weak frication and some formant structure, with a higher F2 than the initial approximant of "west," in keeping with Fuchs' results.

Trudgill et al. (2004) point out that the sound /w/ occurs in 76 per cent of the languages included in Maddieson (1984), while only 21 per cent have /v/, suggesting that the latter is more marked (Trudgill et al. 2004: 222); I would add that only about 1 per cent of these languages have /ʋ/, making it even more marked. Losing the contrast in favor of [w] might indicate a markedness effect, but the survival of [ʋ] suggests other factors are involved. Substrate languages may play a role in contributing the labiodental approximant [ʋ], found in both Indo-Aryan and Dravidian languages, to the IndE system. Many of these languages do not have labiodental fricatives [v]/[f], nor do they distinguish between the labiovelar and labiodental glides [w]/[ʋ]. In many Dravidian languages, for example, the labiodental /ʋ/ has [w] as an allophone in some positions, as in Tamil which has [w] before back round vowels (Nagarajan 1985). Among the three Tibeto-Burman L1s of Wiltshire (2005), Angami has both /w/ and /v/, but Ao has only /w/ and Mizo only /v/. IndE speakers generally maintain a contrast in English, so they have had to acquire a new sound or a new distribution of sounds to make the new contrast.

The presence of [ʋ] in many Indian L1s may have contributed to making it a favorite realization for <v>, as the sound was widely available in the feature pool of substrate languages when English came to India. Furthermore, it may have been in the English pool as well. Although current BrE makes the contrast <v>/<w> using a [v] with frication as demonstrated in Fuchs (2019), earlier speakers of English may have brought a different system to India as Trudgill et al. (2004) describe a merger in varieties of southeastern English in the eighteenth and nineteenth centuries. In some, [v]/[w] were reportedly in

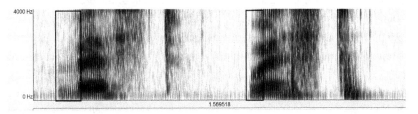

Figure 7 Labiodental vs. labiovelar: "vest", "west" (Chennai-Tamil).

Sound 7 Audio file available at www.cambridge.org/wiltshire

complementary distribution, with [v] post-vocalically (*love*) and [w] initially (*village*), while in others, both merged as a bilabial approximant or fricative, either way resulting in a loss of contrast. Trudgill et al. note that "the merger is a feature which reportedly makes an appearance in the phonologies of a large number of lesser-known colonial varieties of English spoken in small communities in the North Atlantic, South Atlantic, North Pacific and South Pacific" (2004: 214). Their research suggests that any merger was transported by British speakers who had merged the contrast already themselves.

3.2.4 Rhotics

Rhotics in IndE have been investigated for two characteristics: realizations of the rhotic(s) used and whether they are pronounced post-vocalically. For the first, IndE has been described as having a range of realizations, even in descriptions of a model or standard. CIEFL (1972) lists /r/ in the approximant row but say that phonetically the /r/ "may vary from a strong trill (quite rare) through a flap and a fricative to a retroflex or retracted central vowel" (1972: 7), while Bansal (1976) describes it as an approximant or flap and Singh (2004) as a tap or trill. For the use of post-vocalic rhotics, variation is also reported in the percentage of use/absence of potential rhotics, as well as in the range of realizations in post-vocalic positions. I will first discuss the realizations of rhotics and then their use post-vocalically, both of which tend to introduce variability rather than uniformity in IndE.

Types Of Rhotics

Most studies have confirmed that even individual speakers use more than one type of rhotic in their IndE, though most individuals and groups have clear favorites overall. Wiltshire and Harnsberger (2006) found that speakers with Gujarati as an L1 tended to use either taps or trills prevocalically, and taps almost exclusively intervocalically; Tamil speakers most frequently used approximants, though taps were also common, and all used a fricativized approximant at some point, accounting for 12 per cent of the prevocalic tokens (2006: 99). Jose (1992) describes Malayalam English as tending to have approximants finally, flaps after consonants, trills initially, and partially devoiced taps elsewhere (1992: 161). Wiltshire (2015) found that the tap was the most common rhotic for Kannada, Malayalam, and Telugu L1 speakers, though again there was variation even within individuals' speech. Wiltshire (2005) found that Tibeto-Burman IndE speakers generally used an approximant and rarely a tap. Thus, the use of a particular rhotic as a favorite may be an indicator of subvarieties of IndE, but in most cases will require statistical

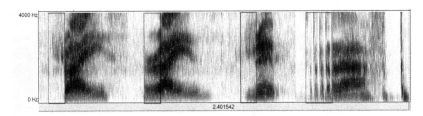

Figure 8 Variability in rhotics: "rice", "rise", "rip" (Mumbai-Marathi), "raft" (Chennai-Tamil).

Sound 8 Audio file available at www.cambridge.org/wiltshire

evaluation over a stretch of speech, rather than being determinable by a short utterance. Figure 8 shows the variability in rhotics used word-initially by one speaker (Mumbai-Marathi) who has a tap, approximant, and slightly fricatized approximant in 'rice', 'rise' and 'rip' respectively; this is followed by an example of a trill from the Chennai-Tamil speaker's production of 'raft'.

Postvocalic Use

Early models allow for both rhotic and non-rhotic varieties of IndE (CIEFL 1972), although some describe IndE as rhotic only (Bansal & Harrison 2013 [1972], Nihalani et al. 1979). Bansal (1990) and Gargesh (2004) describe rhoticity as linguistically conditioned, while others have reported both regional and social variability (Agnihotri & Sahgal 1985, Sharma 2005, Wiltshire 2005, Chand 2010). Descriptions of specific varieties of IndE vary as well. Ghosh (1996) describes Bengali English as generally rhotic, while Maxwell and Fletcher (2010) reported that more productions of their three Hindi and four Punjabi L1 speakers[6] were non-rhotic. The use of post-vocalic <r> is often variable even within varieties traditionally labelled "rhotic" and "non-rhotic," and therefore measured in terms of what percentage of potential post-vocalic rhotics are realized by a population. To understand the typical use of these terms, Chand (2010) provides comparison numbers from other dialects, ranging from "rhotic" varieties such as white speakers in New Hampshire (USA) who pronounce 87 per cent of possible rhotics, to variable rhoticity such as Southern USA with 49 per cent, to a conventional "non-rhotic" variety of New Zealand, where 8 per cent of potential post-vocalic <r> s were realized. Some studies provide percentages of post-vocalic rhotic use, and the varieties of IndE described fit into different categories. Among the non-rhotic are the Gujarati

---

[6] Two of the Punjabi speakers in Maxwell and Fletcher (2009, 2010) began learning English at age ten.

and Tamil L1 speakers of Wiltshire and Harnsberger (2006), who realized 17 per cent and 15 per cent respectively of possible post-vocalic <r> s, while rhotic varieties include Tibeto-Burman IndE speakers, who regularly (83–91 per cent) use post-vocalic [ɹ] (Wiltshire 2005).

Detailed sociophonetic studies have found that speakers in Delhi vary widely, from 12–62 per cent, depending on age and other social factors (Agnihotri & Sahgal 1985, Sahgal & Agnihotri 1988, Chand 2010), though Chand notes that Delhi may not be representative even of large cities in India. The Agihotri and Sahgal (1985) study of South Delhi speakers examined postvocalic <r> against social factors including age, language background, and high school prestige and observed that older generations were more r-full, while younger speakers from more prestigious backgrounds were less rhotic; they also suggest that the use/absence of postvocalic rhotics depends on IndE norms based on social factors, rather than L1 background. Sahgal and Agnihotri (1988) report that for the English-medium educated students in their study, post-vocalic rhotic use was low (12 per cent) while students educated in a local language were more rhotic (62 per cent). Chand's (2010) study recorded twenty-nine upper-middle class Hindi/English bilinguals in New Delhi, ranging from ages eighteen to eighty-seven, in contexts differing in formality and spontaneity, and found an overall tendency toward realizing post-vocalic <r>, with 54.6 per cent approximants and 7.8 per cent trills vs. 37.6 per cent null. However, significant linguistic and social factors favored non-rhoticity: pre-consonantal environments, schwa nuclei, formality, and female gender. Both the formality and the gender results are taken to indicate that less post-vocalic rhoticity use is linked to higher prestige, though Chand notes that the current linguistic landscape, with less emphasis on pronunciation in schooling and more variety in the media, allowed a shift toward more heterogeneity and more rhoticity among the youth. Her overall finding is that post-vocalic rhotic use is age/gender conditioned, to a degree she suggests is greater than that of other potential pan-IndE features. From all this research, there are two general themes: varieties, registers, and speakers differ in their degree of rhoticity, and the relative prestige of rhotic vs. non-rhotic use may be changing.

For both the extent of rhoticity and the types of rhotics used, potential founder effects are unclear, as even British varieties differ. Studies that mention the types of rhotics in current varieties (e.g., Beal 2004) include alveolar, retroflex, and even uvular approximants as well as taps. Dialects both present and past vary in post-vocalic rhoticity as well, and though current RP is non-rhotic post-vocalically, varieties from Scotland and Ireland are generally rhotic (Wells 1982, Melchers & Shaw 2013). For India, non-rhotic RP was not the only prestigious variety, as Chand (2010: 31) writes: "Pre-Partition India was run by Britishers from across the UK – as such there was a range of accents, some non-rhotic and some rhotic. All of these pronunciations were prestigious, given their role as the colonizer's code. As such, Indian speakers of English had multiple prestige targets, in terms of rhoticity."

There is potentially a role for transfer in the type of rhotics preferred in different varieties. Wiltshire and Harnsberger (2006) connect the tendencies of Gujarati speakers to use either taps or trills, with mostly taps in intervocalic position, to the existence of taps in Gujarati. Taps are often mentioned as part of the standard for IndE, and, in fact, many Indian languages have taps in their inventory, including Dravidian Tamil, Telugu, and Malayalam (Krishnamurti 2003) and Indo-Aryan Assamese, Hindi, Bengali, etc. (Masica 1991). While Tamil speakers also use taps in IndE, approximants are most frequent and they also produce the fricativized approximant that is in Tamil itself. The presence of these rhotics may also result from their prevalence in the pool of substrate features. In the northeast, Tibeto-Burman L1 speakers' use of the approximant in Wiltshire (2005) cannot be purely transfer, since of three L1s, only Ao has an approximant yet speakers from all groups use it as their modal rhotic (95–100 per cent when postvocalic, 78–87 per cent when prevocalic). Wiltshire (2005: 286) observes: "this distinct characteristic of TB-IE can be called transfer only for the Ao speakers; the Mizo and Angami do not have an approximant rhotic in their inventories, yet they use it consistently in their English," suggesting a regional norm.

3.3 Overview for Uniformity vs. Variability of Consonants

I have examined place (retroflex, dental), stop voicing/voicelessness, <v/w> realization and contrast, and rhotic realization and use post-vocalically. While there are characteristics that are widely shared across IndE, most also show divergence at the regional, local, or L1 level, or show sociolinguistic sensitivity to age, gender, and formality (Table 4). The one feature widely shared is the prevoicing of voiced stops; I suspect that the realization of the voiceless with "optional" aspiration should be examined more closely to determine whether linguistic, sociolinguistic, or other factors determine the options.

This survey is far from exhaustive, and there are many other aspects of the consonantal system worthy of examination. For example, the alveolar lateral approximant /l/ is often said to be pronounced as clear [l] in all contexts in IndE (e.g. Gargesh 2004, Sailaja 2009), but Bansal (1990) observed that some speakers used velarized (dark) [ɫ] before consonants and word-finally, while both Mohanan and Mohanan (2003) and Sailaja (2009) mention retroflex [ɭ] as well. Furthermore, the phonotactics of IndE deserve more inquiry. It has been claimed

Table 4 Overview for consonants

Widespread uniformity	Variability
Retroflexes (North & South)	Regional: Lack of retroflexion (Northeast)
Dental stops	Sociolinguistic & Linguistic: dental fricatives (formal, post-vocalic, etc.)
/b d g/ Prevoicing	
/p t k/ Aspiration optional	Details of aspiration yet unknown
Existence of <v>/<w> contrast, use of [ʋ]	Extent & Realization of contrast
Modal rhotic: tap	Realization %s (taps, trills, approximants)
	Regional: modal approximant (Northeast)
	Post-vocalic rhoticity/non-rhoticity
	Sociolinguistic & Linguistic: age, gender, formality

that some IndE speakers, generally in the North, epenthesize a vowel into word-initial consonant clusters, especially those beginning with sC (Bansal 1990, Shuja 1995, Gargesh 2008) and in the South, word-initial vowels may trigger epenthesis of an approximant [j] or [w] (Nagarajan 1985, Sailaja 2009). Although I have heard neither of these phenomena in my data, I have observed word-final obstruent devoicing and consonant cluster reduction differing across speakers from Tibeto-Burman and Indo-Aryan L1s (Wiltshire 2017), while Khan (1991) examined factors that favor t/d deletion in final clusters among IndE speakers from U.P. and found that, in addition to occurring more often, t/d deletion follows a distinct pattern in IndE relative to other Englishes. A fuller description and analysis of all the consonants, in systematic, realizational, and distributional terms, will no doubt reveal further uniformities, divergences, and local characteristics. Finally, the sociophonetic research on rhotics (Agnihotri & Sahgal 1985, Sahgal & Agnihotri 1988, Chand 2010) reminds us that, as a living language, IndE characteristics are subject to change over time; a more complete picture of both stability and variation will include a wider range of age-based data.

4 Vowels

As with the consonants, I will present standard descriptions (Section 4.1) and then discuss some major characteristics which either may mark a shared IndE variety or divergence among varieties, and where possible the likely sources of these features (4.2). Finally, I will provide an overview of commonalities and differences (4.3).

4.1 Standard Descriptions of the IndE Vowel System

Again, I start with these general descriptions, used by many studies of IndE varieties looking for conformity or divergence. Previous descriptions have provided some agreement on the expected inventory of a standard IndE vowel system (CIEFL 1972, Nihalani et al. 1979, Wells 1982, Gargesh 2004, Sailaja 2009, Bansal & Harrison 2013 [1972], Pandey 2015), although all allow for alternative pronunciations for at least some of the vowels. According to the CIEFL (1972) version, General Indian English (GIE) has the vowel system shown in Table 5, where the symbols in parentheses are considered acceptable alternate pronunciations, such as [ɛː] for [eː]. One vowel is listed as having optional length [ɒ(ː)], and the open-mid back vowel, whether long or short ([ɔ,ɔː]) is listed as completely optional to the system.

Wells (1982) provides "lexical sets," groups of words that tend to be pronounced with the same vowel within a variety, although across varieties the vowel used for a given lexical set may be different. These lexical sets, indicated with keywords, provide a means to describe vowel systems without prejudging the vowel contrasts or qualities, as well as an easy shorthand for comparisons among dialects.[7] Wells provides a description of IndE using these keywords, which I have organized by backness and height for the monophthongs provided in Table 6, in order to compare with Table 5. Wells' monophthongal inventory proves similar to that of Table 5, with the exception of not marking length on the tense [i e u o] vowels, as Wells claims that "length distinctions, however, are not always consistently made" (1982: 626).

The remaining diphthongs and potential vowel+rhotic combinations from Wells are given in Table 7. For sets that list the rhotic as optional, the non-rhotic pronunciation is always the same as some monophthong in Table 6 (e.g., words in the FORCE set may be pronounced with [o] as in GOAT).

Table 5 CIEFL's GIE monophthongs (CIEFL 1972: 6)

Height	Front	Central	Back
Close	iː		uː
	ɪ		ʊ
Close-mid	eː (ɛː)	ər (ɜːr) ə	oː
Open-mid	ɛ		(ɔ,ɔː)
Open	æ	aː (ɑː)	ɒ(ː)

---

[7] Keywords of the Wells sets, as pronounced by four of the speakers used for illustrative purposes here, are provided in the Supplemental Resources on-line.

Table 6 Wells' monophthongs of IndE (Wells 1982: 626)

Height	Front		Central		Back	
Close	FLEECE	i			GOOSE	u
	KIT	ɪ			FOOT	ʊ
	HAPP*Y*	i, ɪ				
Close-mid	FACE	e			GOAT	o
Open-mid	DRESS	ɛ	STRUT	ʌ, ə [+]	THOUGHT	ɔ [++]
			COMM*A*	a, ə	CLOTH	ɒ,ɔ
Open	TRAP	æ	BATH	a [+++]	LOT	ɒ
			PALM	a		

[+] phonemic status not clear: may be allophones of /ə/ or independent phoneme /ʌ/

[++] or /ɒ/ for those who lack /ɔ/

[+++] or sometimes /æ/

Table 7 Wells' diphthongs & potential rhotic combinations in IndE (Wells 1982: 626)

Height (1st vowel)	Front		Central		Back	
Close	NEAR	ɪə(r)			CURE	ʊə(r) [++]
Close-mid	SQUARE	eə(r)	LETT*ER*	ə(r)	FORCE	o(r) [++]
Open-mid			NURSE	ər or ʌr [+]	CHOICE	ɔɪ
Open			PRICE	aɪ	NORTH	ɒ(r) or ɔ(r)
			MOUTH	aʊ	START	ɑ(r)

[+] or, less commonly, /ɜ/

[++] or [oə(r)]; occasionally [ɔə(r)]

In addition to differences about length, general descriptions also diverge on the question of rhoticity as addressed in Section 3.2.4. For vowel+rhotic combinations, CIEFL (1972) generally lists pronunciations with the rhotic present and provides differing diphthong realizations to be discussed in Section 4.2.4. Where there are further discrepancies among descriptions of standards, those will be mentioned in the appropriate subsection.

Sharma (2005: 208) claims that vowel systems vary more than consonants in IndE subvarieties; given that the standard descriptions do not entirely agree, and even internally contain a great deal of variability and optionality, we might expect that the vowel system will primarily be a source of variability for IndE. Description of individual "varieties" based on L1 abound, noting specific differences in the vowel systems and their realizations (e.g., Balasubramanian 1972, Nagarajan 1985, Jose 1992, Ghosh 1996, Rajalakshmi 2008, etc.). As with the consonants, rather than discussing every possible aspect of the phonemic system and its realization, I have chosen a subset to discuss here.

4.2 Potential Characteristics of IndE Varieties

This section focuses on some vowel contrasts and realizations that are widely reported as either distinct throughout IndE compared with other Englishes or as differing among IndE subvarieties. I begin with several comparisons of lexical sets, examining descriptions of IndE vowels and their productions by specific groups of speakers to evaluate both the realizations of vowels and the distinctions maintained between lexical sets (Sections 4.2.1–4.2.4). I then discuss some general system-wide characteristics: length vs. quality distinctions and vowel reduction (Section 4.2.5).

4.2.1 Long Mid-Vowels: FACE and GOAT

I begin with two lexical sets for which descriptions agree, the mid-vowels of FACE and GOAT, both of which are reportedly realized by monophthongs [e:] and [o:] (e.g. Bansal 1983, Sailaja 2009, Pandey 2015) or short [e] and [o] (in Wells 1982). There are rare mentions of any variation in quality, as when CIEFL (1972) allows for [e:] to be pronounced as [ɛ:] and Gargesh (2004) reports that [o:] is sometimes pronounced as [ɔ:], but all agree that these mid-vowels are monophthongal.

Acoustic studies measuring vowel quality in terms of formant values (F1 and F2) have documented the quality of these vowels and their monophthongal nature in a wide variety of IndE speakers, most organized by L1 groups in these studies. The quality of the FACE vowel as [e] and that of GOAT as [o] has been found in the productions of IndE speakers from L1 backgrounds of the Indo-Aryan languages Hindi, Punjabi (Maxwell & Fletcher 2009, 2010), and Gujarati (Wiltshire & Harnsberger 2006), the Dravidian languages Malayalam (Nair 1996) and Tamil (Nagarajan 1985, Wiltshire & Harnsberger 2006), and the Tibeto-Burman languages Angami, Ao and Mizo (Wiltshire 2005). While GOAT was uniformly monophthongal among their three Hindi and four Punjabi L1 speakers, Maxwell and Fletcher (2010) found a few diphthongal productions for FACE (as [eɪ]) from an individual Punjabi L1 speaker, though the majority of speakers and productions were monophthongs. Measures of duration in Wiltshire and Harnsberger (2006) and Maxwell and Fletcher (2009) for their speakers of Tamil, Gujarati, Hindi, and Punjabi support the transcription as long. Individual varieties may lack

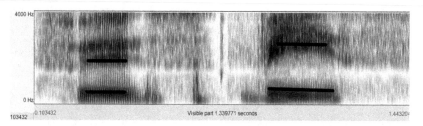

Figure 9 Monophthongal FACE vowel in "face" (Chennai-Tamil), "vase" (Mumbai-Marathi).

Sound 9 Audio file available at www.cambridge.org/wiltshire

length contrasts in general (Section 4.2.5), but it seems that these vowels are long in any variety that uses length.

Figure 9 illustrates the monophthongal FACE vowel in "face" and "vase" by the Chenai-Tamil male and Mumbai-Marathi female speaker, while the GOAT vowel appeared earlier in Figure 5. The F1 and F2 are relatively stable throughout the vowel, moving only at the edges for transitions to consonants.

Three potential sources favor monophthongal realizations for the FACE and GOAT vowels: transfer, markedness, and founder varieties. Many, if not all, of the L1s of the subjects evaluated previously have [e] and [o] quality monophthongs, and most, if not all, lack mid-vowel diphthongs (Masica 1991, Krishnamurti 2003). Markedness favors monophthongs as well, as being structurally simpler than diphthongs (Wiltshire 2014). Last, but definitely not least, the monopthongal pronunciations for FACE and GOAT words were certainly present in the pool of English varieties available during the formation of IndE. Diphthongization of the mid-vowels happened around 1800 in the precursor to BrEng RP, according to Wells (1982), which means that earlier forms of even the most prestigious varieties used [eː] and [oː] monophthongs. Furthermore, the mid-vowels never became diphthongs in many places, including "rural and conservative urban working-class accents of the north of England; rather more generally in Wales and Ireland; very generally in Scotland" (Wells 1982: 211). With these monophthongs in the Englishes brought to India, present in substrates, and favored by markedness, it is unsurprising that monophthongal vowels in FACE and GOAT are widespread. The only factor that might favor diphthongal pronunciations is from exonormative models such as modern standard AmE and RP, which clearly have not prevailed over the combined forces favoring monophthongs.

4.2.2 Back Open/Open-Mid Vowels: LOT, THOUGHT (CLOTH)

Unlike FACE and GOAT, descriptions of LOT, THOUGHT, and CLOTH vowels are widely conflicting and variable. Wells (1982: 626) lists LOT as [ɒ], CLOTH as [ɒ,ɔ], and THOUGHT as [ɔ] with a footnote clarifying that it may also be "/ɒ/ for those who lack /ɔ/." This suggests speakers can pronounce all three classes with [ɒ] or make a two-way distinction, [ɒ] vs. [ɔ], with CLOTH words pronounced either way. As Wells does not indicate length, there is also the possibility of making a three-way contrast using two qualities, one having long and short variants. Others claim that LOT-THOUGHT are either merged (Bansal 1990) or distinguished by length rather than quality (LOT short, THOUGHT long) (Nihalani et al. 1979: 209, Gargesh 2008: 233; Sailaja 2009: 25). There is little discussion of CLOTH vowels, and I have found no acoustical reports on its quality.

Many describe a lack of any [ɔ] vowel. Normally, /ɔ:/ is said to be replaced by /ɒ:/ but /o(:)/ or even /a/ are also mentioned as possibilities (CIEFL 1972, Nihalani et al. 1979, Bansal 1983, Gargesh 2004); Sailaja (2009) also suggests that /a/ is used for /ɒ/, which she finds "particularly true of south Indian Tamil, Kannada and Telugu speech" (Sailaja 2009: 25), while Domange (2015: 536) describes THOUGHT as "occasionally realised as [ɐ] when the spelling comports to <a>" (e.g. *water*, *salt*)." The [ɔ] vowel has been also described an allophone available for sociolinguistic purposes. Sailaja (2009) describes it as limited to those with special pronunciation training, and sometimes heard on All-India Radio, while Sahgal and Agnihotri (1988) found /ɔ:/ use higher among those of their Delhi middle-class speakers based on schooling (English-medium), style (reading/formal), gender (female) and age (younger), suggesting it is the prestige variant. Even in formal style by English-medium speakers, however, its use was 64.8 per cent, while in the casual speech of vernacular-medium speakers it was only 19.5 per cent.

In acoustic research, Wiltshire (2005) found a LOT-THOUGHT merger for the L1 speakers of Tibeto-Burman languages, though the quality of vowel used for its realization differed; for L1 Mizo speakers it was [ɔ], while for L1 Ao and Angami, the vowel's quality fell between [o] and [ɔ]. Wiltshire and Harnsberger (2006), found little difference in the averaged production of the back vowels /ɑ:/ and /ɔ:/ for both Gujarati and Tamil L1 groups. Examining the individual speaker data underlying that report, I find that four of the five Gujarati speakers seemed to have merged the LOT-THOUGHT words to /ɔ:/, while one has a lower LOT vowel than THOUGHT. Each of the Tamil speakers has likely merged LOT-THOUGHT as well, but to qualities ranging from low /ɒ/ to low-mid /ɔ/. Both works omitted CLOTH words from examination, but rechecking the data for the two CLOTH words it contained (*cloth*, *odd*) revealed that all groups used vowels ranging from [o] to [ɔ] in quality. The Gujarati group tended to produce both words with /ɔ/, but the Tamil group varies by word and speaker. It appears that speakers have assigned these two CLOTH words to either the LOT-THOUGHT or GOAT sets on an individual basis. Looking at the values for individual Tamil speakers, one uses /ɔ/ for LOT-THOUGHT and a vowel near /o/ in quality for CLOTH, while another uses an /ɒ/ quality for LOT-THOUGHT and /ɔ/ for CLOTH. Thus, there is no uniformity in the vowel's realization within these sets of speakers, but most do merge LOT-THOUGHT.

Maxwell and Fletcher (2009) report a difference between LOT and THOUGHT for their Hindi and Punjabi L1 speakers, and list LOT as [ɔ]. However, as Domange (2015) points out, there is an issue with their THOUGHT tokens, as they mistakenly treated the token *horde* (a FORCE word) as a NORTH word instead (Maxwell & Fletcher 2009: 58) and, furthermore "[i]n the absence of a THOUGHT token in their Australian National Database of Spoken Language (ANDOSL) list, they seem to extend their results for NORTH to the THOUGHT class" (Domange 2015: 536). The result attributed to THOUGHT is therefore actually the vowel of FORCE, so we can draw no conclusions about any LOT/THOUGHT merger or contrast.

Domange (2015) analyzed the formants and durations of LOT and THOUGHT words, with GOAT also for comparison, produced by the ten speakers from Delhi mentioned in Section 3.2.1. He compares the vowels of the three sets, and determines that THOUGHT/GOAT and LOT/GOAT are signficantly different for all speakers, but THOUGHT/LOT are not. The quality of merged LOT/THOUGHT is a low or mid-low back slightly rounded vowel [ɒ], differing from GOAT's [o] quality, especially in the F1 value indicating a lower vowel height. Domange also performs durational measures and comparisons. The ratios of duration of LOT:GOAT and LOT:THOUGHT are in both cases near 1:1, while a comparison set KIT: FLEECE is shown to be 1:1.7; thus Domange concludes that in addition to sharing a quality, LOT and THOUGHT share a quantity, being long like GOAT, and are realized as [ɒː].

This set of words has indicated very little uniformity, except that the described lack of contrast between LOT-THOUGHT has been supported by acoustic research in several groups: the Hindi speakers of Domange (2015), the Ao, Angami, and Mizo speakers of Wiltshire (2005), and nine of ten of the Gujarati and Tamil speakers of Wiltshire and Harnsberger (2006). The quality of this vowel may vary, from mid-close to open, as [o], [ɔ], or [ɒ], and this variation may be based on groups, individuals, or sociolinguistic factors.

Figure 10 provides an example of "cloth", "thought", and "lot" from the Tinsukia-Assamese speaker, with formants highlighted. The lower F1 of "cloth" shows that it is higher, like GOAT in quality; the quality of this specific word may be influenced by analogy to the GOAT vowel in *clo_thing*. For this speaker, "thought" and "lot" share their quality, having a lower vowel (higher F1 bar) and less rounding.

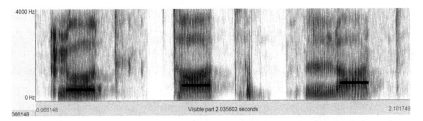

Figure 10 "cloth", "thought", "lot" (Tinsukia-Assamese).
Sound 10 Audio file available at www.cambridge.org/wiltshire

A lack of contrast between the LOT/THOUGHT classes can be found among the varieties of English brought to India, especially Scottish (Wells 1982, Domange 2015). Wells (1982: 399) in fact reports all three (LOT/CLOTH/THOUGHT) are merged in Scottish with an [ɔ] pronunciation.

While suggesting that such speakers could have influenced the transmission of this feature to IndE, Domange (2015: 554) also notes that it could also have "emerged from substrate-driven innovative linguistic behaviours (given a standardised British English input)."

4.2.3 Contrast in NORTH, FORCE

Wells (1982: 626) reports that "[i]n what from an RP point of view is a striking archaism, the historical distinction between the lexical sets FORCE and NORTH is maintained"; he lists [ɒ(r) ~ ɔ(r)] for NORTH and [o(r)] for FORCE. Wells also claims that "FORCE almost invariably has a vowel phonemically identical with that of GOAT" for varieties which have not merged FORCE and NORTH (1982: 161). Gargesh (2008) describes NORTH as largely [ɔ], while FORCE is mostly [o], both potentially variable. A similar observation can be found in Bansal and Harrison 2013 [1972] and Bansal (1983), who mention that /ɒ/ is used in *horse* (a NORTH word), while /oː/ is used in *force*, thus agreeing that there is a distinction but differing in realizations. Their descriptions also have /ɒ/ for *hot* (a LOT word), suggesting that NORTH/LOT are merged. On the other hand, several descriptions of the standard do not mention the distinction or give any examples, such as Nihalani et al. (1979), while Sailaja (2009: 27) mentions that *court* (a FORCE word) with /oː/ contrasts with LOT /ɒ/ and TAUGHT /ɒː/, but provides no examples of a NORTH word.

Wiltshire (2005) and Wiltshire and Harnsberger (2006) failed to include any words from the NORTH and FORCE lexical sets. As already mentioned, Maxwell and Fletcher (2009) measured a word from the FORCE set and reported its value as /oː/, but mislabeled it as a NORTH word; as they did not measure any NORTH words we cannot verify whether their speakers made any contrast. Fortunately, Domange (2011, 2015) focused on this distinction, drawing on the same research with ten speakers in South Delhi mentioned in Sections 3.2.1 and 4.2.2. In addition to the GOAT, LOT, and THOUGHT vowels discussed in Section 4.2.2, he measured the formants and duration of the vowels used in NORTH and FORCE words in both spontaneous and read speech. Domange finds that his speakers do maintain the distinction between open and mid-close back rounded vowels in the NORTH and FORCE sets, with the vowel of NORTH words lower than those of FORCE words; both vowels are comparable in duration to each other, and similar to the length of other long vowels in the system by comparison to the FLEECE/KIT words of the same speakers. This suggests a transcription of NORTH as [ɒː] vs. FORCE as [oː], giving NORTH words the same vowel as LOT/THOUGHT words.

How widespread is this distinction, and is it a candidate for a shared feature of IndE? I examined tokens of NORTH and FORCE words (three each) from the data gathered in 2003 in Hyderabad from five speakers each of L1s Angami, Ao, Bengali, Hindi, Kannada, and Malayalam, and with Priyankoo Sarmah, analyzed our 2019 data from ten Assamese speakers (ten NORTH, four FORCE tokens each); as before, all tokens were taken from recordings of word list readings. Table 8 reports formant values for the two classes, where F1 is inversely correlated with height and F2 directly with backness. As the samples were small, the F1 and F2 of each lexical class were compared with each other for significance using Student's t-test.

Like Domange, I found variability, particularly in the realization of the vowel in *war*, included in the 2003 data. Nonetheless, speakers of Assamese, Bengali, Kannada, and Malayalam uniformly made the distinction in both F1 and F2, while Hindi and Angami speakers used distinct F1; speakers used an [oː] in

Table 8 Average formant values for NORTH vs. FORCE words

L1 (number of speakers)	NORTH F1 (Hz)	NORTH F2 (Hz)	FORCE F1 (Hz)	FORCE F2 (Hz)	Significant at p<.05? F1	F2
Angami (5)	635	1,017	528	930	yes	no
Ao (5)	665	1,139	582	1,006	no	no
Assamese (10)	634	1,019	509	884	yes	yes
Bengali (5)	658	997	464	890	yes	yes
Hindi (5)	600	934	507	853	yes	no
Kannada (5)	673	1,045	494	896	yes	yes
Malayalam (5)	653	1,038	489	848	yes	yes

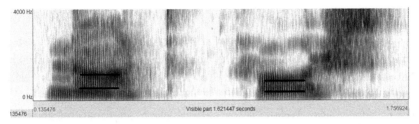

Figure 11 Contrast between "north" vs. "force" (Mysore-Kannada)
Sound 11 Audio file available at www.cambridge.org/wiltshire

FORCE words and a lower vowel ([ɔː~ɒː]) in NORTH words. Ao speakers overall did not distinguish the two, and a few individual speakers from other groups did not appear to use it for all lexical items either. This distinction appears to be widespread, but not perhaps completely uniform.

As an example, Figure 11 shows "north" and "force" spoken by the Mysore-Kannada speaker, with formants highlighted. The vowel of "force" is higher (lower F1) and resembles that of GOAT.

A major argument of Domange's work is that features of the vowel inventory of IndE can often be traced to founder varieties rather than some kind of transfer in current L2 acquisition. While current RP lacks the contrast between NORTH-FORCE, Domange notes that forms of Southern English differed over the contact period with India, and that varieties further afield in Great Britain did and still do differ; Standard Scottish English speakers maintain the distinction between NORTH and FORCE vowels and the identity between GOAT and FORCE today (Domange 2015: 553). Domange concludes that "the 'non-standard' input stands out as the most plausible explanation, for at least two reasons. First, the presence of Scottish and Irish speakers was significant, notably at the front line of language transmission. Second, the fact that their input was maintained up until the end of the colonial period leaves more chronological latitude for establishing sufficient stabilisation of IE" (2015: 553–4).

Education may also perpetuate the contrast. Sharma (2017) notes that the distinction of [oː] vs. [ɔː] is documented in Anglo-Indian speech (Coelho 1997), and suggests that the "distinction appears in the speech of some general Indian English speakers as well, possibly transmitted through convent education" (Sharma 2017: 316). Also reinforcing this distinction, Domange (2015) points out, is the influence of English orthography, as "the spelling of the words often provides an indication of whether they belong to one class or the other ... It is thus conceivable, even quite likely, that spelling has played a significant role in the maintenance of the distinction, particularly <oa> which clearly indicates identity between the vowels in GOAT and FORCE words" (2015: 550).

4.2.4 Diphthongs and Vowels+Rhotics: Price Mouth Choice Near Square Cure

These are gathered in one section because, although we have numerous and varied descriptions of their pronunciations, there is little acoustic research bearing on their phonetic realization; only Maxwell and Fletcher (2010) have measured the acoustic quality and duration of the entire set. Previous descriptions generally match Wells (1982) in treating these as six distinct categories in IndE, with minor differences that may be varietal or idiosyncratic. CIEFL (1972) gives rhotic versions and lists diphthongs beginning with tense vowels for NEAR ([iər]~[iːr]), CURE ([uər]~[uːr]), and SQUARE ([eər]~[eːr]). For CHOICE, CIEFL agrees with Wells ([ɔɪ]), but for PRICE and MOUTH provides options for them to begin with a schwa, as [aɪ]~[əɪ] and [aʊ]~[əʊ]. Maxwell and Fletcher (2010) give further examples of varying past descriptions, including: "The diphthong /ɔɪ/, as in CHOICE, can be realized as [ɒɪ],[ɔːɪ], [ɔɛ] (Nihalani et al. 2004, Bansal 1983), [oe] or [oɪ] (Gargesh 2004)" (2010: 29).

In their study, Maxwell and Fletcher measure the six lexical sets produced by three Hindi and four Punjabi L1 speakers, finding a great deal of variation which they suggest may be due to different levels of education, proficiency, and/or L1 group. I present their findings of realizations of the lexical classes (Table 9) in terms of shared pronunciations and additional ones produced only within one L1 group, with Wells (1982) for comparison. Matching previous accounts, there were generally six distinct pronunciations for the six classes, except that some Punjabi speakers used [iə] always for NEAR and sometimes for SQUARE as well, indicating potential mergers. Maxwell and Fletcher found that only PRICE, NEAR, and SQUARE were diphthongal for all speakers in the study. A few descriptions have included non-diphthongal pronunciations for CURE and SQUARE (Bansal 1990, Gargesh 2004), but monophthongal alternatives appeared among the realizations

Table 9 Realization of diphthongs from Maxwell and Fletcher (2010)

Lexical set	Shared pronunciations	Additional only by Hindi L1	Additional only by Punjabi L1	Wells 1982
PRICE	[ɑɪ]	[ʙɪ]	[ai] [ʙi]	aɪ
MOUTH	[ɑu]		[ʙo][ɑː]	aʊ
CHOICE	[ɒ]	[ɔɪ][ɒɪ]	[oe][oː]	ɔɪ
NEAR	[iə]			ɪə
SQUARE	[eə]	[ɪə]	[iə]	eə
CURE(TOUR)	[uː][uə]			ʊə (ɔə, ɔə)

for three classes (MOUTH, CHOICE, CURE), and "none of the speakers produced the full set of diphthongal vowels proposed in the literature" (Maxwell & Fletcher 2010: 41). Although nowhere was a monophthong the only option, the monophthongs used here ([ɒ] [oː] [uː]) appear elsewhere in the IndE system, suggesting partial mergers with lexical classes such as LOT/NORTH, GOAT, and GOOSE.

Only the NEAR and CURE rows have identical sets of pronunciations for all speakers, but all rows allow for at least one shared pronunciation. Thus, there seems to be uniformity in that some pronunciations are shared across speakers but variation in the range of pronunciations which are not shared. Further research on the phonetics of these pronunciations is needed before we could hazard any further generalizations, but given the variation found within this small groups of speakers, the variability described in previous research seems likely to be validated by further study.

4.2.5 System-Wide Features

As mentioned in Section 4.1, CIEFL (1972) and Wells (1982) differ on whether length is used systematically; furthermore, there are reports that length, rather than quality, replaces some tense-lax distinctions for some speakers/varieties, suggesting variability across IndE. A second potentially systematic feature is the preservation of quality/quantity distinctions in unstressed positions, often called a "lack of vowel reduction," which may characterize IndE uniformly.

The use of length to contrast vowels has been reported to vary among groups and individual IndE speakers (Wells 1982, Gargesh 2004). Standard descriptions often include length on some vowels; for example, Sailaja (2009) describes seven vowels as long /iː eː aː ɒː oː uː ɜː/, though noting that rhotic varieties have /ər/ instead of /ɜː/. However, there are also claims that some varieties of IndE lack length distinctions; for example, Mahanta (2001) describes Assamese English as lacking length altogether, while Datta (1972–3) describes Bengali speakers as using length randomly in English. Bengali English may also have developed a new pattern; Ghosh (1996) describes vowels as uniformly long in monosyllables in Bengali English due to a Bengali minimality requirement, so that English *full* and *fool* are identically long.

Both Wiltshire and Harnsberger (2006) and Maxwell and Fletcher (2009) provide duration measures supporting the existence of length contrasts between tense-lax vowel pairs in the IndE of their Gujarati, Tamil, Hindi, and Punjabi L1 speakers. Wiltshire and Harnsberger (2006) found both Tamil and Gujarati L1 speakers have long-short contrasts for some tense-lax vowels, for example FLEECE-KIT and FACE-DRESS; on the other hand, durational differences between GOOSE-FOOT and START-STRUT vowels were smaller, so length may not be used consistently throughout the entire system. Maxwell and Fletcher (2009) found that the pairs FLEECE-KIT, GOOSE-FOOT, and START-STRUT differ significantly in duration for most speakers, and they provided numerical measures of duration that make it appear that FACE-DRESS is likely different as well. Wiltshire (2005) and (2015) also provide measures of the durations of monophthongs that suggest that Mizo, Kannada, Malayalam Tamil, and Telugu also use length contrasts, while Ao and Angami L1 speakers do not, especially for the aforementioned pairs. The data was not analyzed statistically, but does suggest that not all speakers or varieties make contrasts in length for all tense-lax contrasts.

Payne and Maxwell (2018) investigate the potential contrast of duration between tense-lax vowels in both stressed and unstressed positions in IndE based on two speakers each from four L1 backgrounds, Bengali, Hindi, Tamil, and Telugu. They found durational differences between tense and lax vowel were made by all speakers except the L1 Bengali speakers; both speakers did not distinguish the duration of tense/lax vowels in unstressed positions, and one did not distinguish them in stressed positions either. This may be general for Bengali IndE, as previous descriptions suggested, but it also raises the issue of whether both Bengali speakers were representative, as one did make a contrast in stressed positions like the other IndE speakers.

Where length is used, it may enhance or replace quality distinctions for tense/lax vowels. The front close vowels (FLEECE-KIT) and back close vowels (GOOSE-FOOT) should, according to CIEFL (1972), contrast in both quality and duration, as [iː]-[ɪ] and [uː]-[ʊ], while Wells includes quality but not quantity distinctions ([i]-[ɪ], [u]-[ʊ]). There may be a split in the realization of these contrasts, with some varieties using both quality and quantity, producing [iː] vs. [ɪ] (Hindi & Punjabi in Maxwell & Fletcher 2009, Tamil and Gujarati in Wiltshire & Hansberger 2006), and others using quantity alone, producing [iː] vs. [i] (Mizo, Wiltshire 2005). A third type has been attested, in which the same short tense vowel is used for both; for example, Angami and Ao merge FLEECE/KIT as [i] (Wiltshire 2005). Similarly for the back close vowels of GOOSE and FOOT: varieties contrast [uː] vs. [ʊ] (Tamil in Wiltshire & Harnsberger 2006, most Hindi & Punjabi in Maxwell & Fletcher 2009), [uː] vs. [u] (Gujarati in Wiltshire & Harnsberger 2006), or use [u] for both (Angami, Ao, and Mizo in Wiltshire 2005). Although they did not provide duration measures, the quality differences between tense-lax high vowels also is apparent for the Hindi and Telugu speakers of Sirsa and Redford (2013). Figure 12 shows an example from the Mysore-Kannada speaker who uses both quality and quantity to distinguish FOOT-GOOSE vowels, with the vowels indicated by boxes. The formants of the vowel in "good," a FOOT word, show a lower (higher F1) and

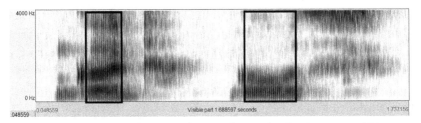

Figure 12 Lax-tense and short-long differences in "good", "goose" (Mysore-Kannada)

Sound 12 Audio file available at www.cambridge.org/wiltshire

more front (larger F2-F1 difference) quality, as well as a shorter duration, than the formants of the vowel in "goose."

If the mergers are related to second language acquisition, then markedness and transfer again both favor choosing tense over lax vowels. Tense high vowels [i] and [u] are less marked than lax high vowels [ɪ] and [ʊ] (Wiltshire 2014), and many Indian L1s have [i] and [u] but lack [ɪ] and [ʊ] in their inventories. As for the Englishes brought to India, Scottish and Ulster English merge GOOSE/FOOT to [u] (Wells 1982, Melchers & Shaw 2013: 66), while merger of KIT/FLEECE to [i] has been described for English in Ireland, Shetland, and Orkney (Schneider 2004), meaning tense vowels were perhaps more densely represented in the pool of features from both substrates and English varietal contributions. As for length, most Indo-Aryan and Dravidian languages use length to distinguish vowels (Masica 1991, Krishnamurti 2003), with the notable exceptions being Bengali and Assamese. Tibeto-Burman languages also vary: Ao and Angami have no vowel length contrasts (Gurubasave-Gowda 1972, Ravindran 1974), while Mizo does (Chhangte 1986).

Turning to vowel reduction, a widespread observation about IndE is that full vowels may appear in unstressed positions, with "full" in the sense of both quality and duration (e.g., CIEFL 1972, Coelho 1997, Pandey 2015). Any lack of vowel reduction in unstressed syllables does not change the IndE vowel system, but can affect its prosodic character, especially rhythm, so discussion of durational differences in stressed vs. unstressed syllables is reserved for the rhythm section (Section 5.3). In terms of vowel quality, CIEFL (1972) noted that "vowels other than /ɪ/ and /ə/ are common in unstressed syllables" (CIEFL 1972: 7), a claim that has been made both in general for IndE (Bansal & Harrison 2013[1972] through Pandey 2015) and in specific for various L1 groups, for example, for Tamil English (Nagarajan 1985). In phonetic research, Saha and Mandal (2016, 2017) support the claim in their examination of twenty L1 Bengali speakers, measuring features, including vowel quality, in stressed vs. unstressed vowels. Overall cues to differentiate stressed from unstressed syllables were generally weak, and Saha and Mandal singled out the tendency of their speakers to not reduce vowel quality in unstressed syllables (2017: 1).

The preservation of vowel quality distinctions in unstressed positions has been attributed to spelling pronunciations (Bansal & Harrison 2013[1972], Nair 1996), which in turn are often attributed to the emphasis on written rather than spoken English in education. However, preserving distinctions of vowel quality can also serve a communicative purpose, making an intended word more distinct. Jenkins, whose work focuses on designing a lingua franca version of English for international use, specifically advises against reducing vowels and using weak forms of function words: "the full vowel sounds tend to help rather than hinder intelligibility" (Jenkins 2002: 98). Especially in conversations involving speakers of different backgrounds and varieties, likely in urban settings, the advantages of preserving full vowels in unstressed positions may help this characteristic of pronunciation to survive.

4.3 Vowel Overview for Uniformity vs. Variability

Previous research on vowel systems in IndE has tended to draw on the L1s of the speakers for explanations of similarities and differences, but as Domange (2015) suggests, the origins of the IndE accent(s) and its current norms play a role. Similarities that are widely shared were generally available in the feature pool of variants from the earliest days of English in India, apart from the lack of reduction of vowel quality in unstressed syllables. Speakers of a variety of L1 backgrounds have acquired vowels and contrasts that are not in their first languages, as noted in Wiltshire and Harnsberger (2006), Maxwell and Fletcher (2009), and Sirsa and Redford (2013), meaning that transfer is not the whole story behind the features that are widely shared, though it can contribute to local divergences. Sirsa & Redford (2013) did not follow the lexical sets approach, but present an overview of monophthongs produced in English and their L1s by Hindi and Telugu speakers (seven each). Comparing the formants of vowels in the L1 and IndE productions, they found that IndE "does vary somewhat with speaker background, but the differences between IE and the native languages are more striking" (2013: 399). For example, the KIT vowel /ɪ/ is higher in Hindi than in Telugu, but the two groups produced the vowel in IndE more centralized than in either of their L1s, similarly to each other.

A brief overview of the vowel features discussed appears in Table 10. As with the consonants, both the research I review here and the way I have organized it

Table 10 Overview for vowels

Widespread Uniformity	Variability
FACE & GOAT monophthongs	
LOT & THOUGHT merger	Realization of the vowel
NORTH vs. FORCE distinction	Not all speakers, & may have lexical and local variation
System of diphthongs	Realization of diphthongs
Use of length for contrast	Regional: contrast only length or only quality
Use of quality for contrast	Local: Bengali, Ao, Angami use neither quality/quantity
Vowel quality maintained in unstressed positions	

tend to fit into preconceived categories and may be missing further factors leading to characteristics worthy of investigation as features of uniformity or variability.

Maxwell and Fletcher (2009: 54) observe that "[p]revious research demonstrates that major differences are found in the realization of back vowels," and I have not much discussed the front vowel system, although differences are reported in both the contrasts and the realizations of front vowels by L1 and region (Wiltshire 2005, Wiltshire & Harnsberger 2006, Maxwell & Fletcher 2009). Furthermore, Domange (2020) provides apparent-time evidence to document a change in progress among the short front vowels of Delhi English speakers, where the TRAP and DRESS vowels are lowering and the KIT vowel shows age-related allophonic variation. He argues that the lowering is a chain shift motivated by linguistic factors internal to the dialect, and he finds parallel changes in other English varieties. Both of these observations raise the possibility that similar changes may be in progress elsewhere in IndE accents and remind us again of the necessity for more sociophonetic research to identify uniformity and variability within IndE.

5 Suprasegmentals

The term suprasegmental applies to characteristics that span a larger stretch of speech than individual consonants and vowels, such as stress, intonation, and rhythm. Suprasegmentals contribute to the sound of IndE (Fuchs 2015) and have long attracted attention from researchers, though at first only to point out differences from external norms that might hamper intelligibility. In an article otherwise focused on vowel qualities in Tamil speakers and their IndE, Balasubramanian (1972: 33) asserts that "[i]t is in matters of stress, rhythm, and intonation that the spoken English of Tamil speakers is particularly defective." There are many similar commentaries on "unintelligible" or "defective" features, but more recent research examines IndE prosody as its own system, and finds commonalities across IndE varieties. As there are no established standards for IndE suprasegmentals, I next present findings on stress (Section 5.1), intonation (Section 5.2) and rhythm (Section 5.3), treating each separately although the phonetic characteristics involved, duration, intensity, and pitch, interact in all three.

5.1 Stress

Stress has two aspects, each of which provides some uniformity in IndE accents: the location of stress within a word (systematic, Section 5.1.1) and its acoustic characteristics (realizational, Section 5.1.2).

5.1.1 Location of stress

Leaving aside works that, as with prosody more generally, treat the location of stress in IndE in terms of "deviations" from other varieties, a fairly substantial body of work attempts to formulate systems of stress placement in IndE varieties, including Vijayakrishnan (1978), Pandey (1980), Nair (1996), Das (2001), and Mahanta (2001), on Tamil, Hindustani, Malayalam, Tripura Bangla, and Assamese English, respectively. Two generalizations emerge from these. First, IndE tends to place stress on the basis of segments and syllable structures, rather than lexical or grammatical distinctions; that is, regardless of grammatical category, IndE stresses heavier syllables near the end of the word. Vijayakrishnan (1978), for example, formulates rules for Tamil English that stress a final syllable with a tense vowel or with a lax vowel followed by a cluster of consonants, thus relying on syllable weight alone. Tibeto-Burman IndE follows the same tendencies of basing stress on syllable size, with stress on a final syllable only if it ends with -V:CC as in *irritates*, on the penult when that syllable ends with a consonant or has a long vowel, as in *December*, *detainee*, and otherwise the antepenult, as in *organize*, *economic* (Wiltshire 2005). Gargesh (2008) provides similar rules, noting that stress also applies to monosyllables, resulting in stress on function as well as content words. A second tendency is to keep stress on the same syllable in related words, such as a base word and suffixed form; CIEFL (1972) mentions this "analogical regularizing" as responsible for stresses in related words like *photograph~photographer* (1972: 7). I observed this also in Tibeto-Burman IndE speakers who tend to stress words with suffixes on the same syllable as the base: *economic~econo-mical* [i.ˈkɔ:.nɔ.mi.kəl], and *person~personify* (Wiltshire 2005: 295).

The reliance on syllable size alone results in two-syllable noun–verb pairs in IndE being stressed on the same syllable (*transfer*N,V, *produce*N,V), an IndE pattern that has been widely observed (Shuja 1995, Mahanta 2001, Gargesh 2008, Pandey 2015) and differs from other varieties that stress nouns initially and verbs finally (*produce*N, *produce*V). Pandey (2015) also notes that in words of three or more syllables, Hindi speakers locate primary stress on either of two specific locations. Fuchs and Maxwell (2015) examined the position of stress in three and four syllable noun–verb pairs produced by L1 Hindi and Malayalam speakers (four each) and found that the dominant pattern was to stress verbs on the antepenult (*calculate* 81 per cent) rather than final syllable (*calculate* 19 per cent), while nouns were more often stressed on the penult (*calculation* 61 per cent) than on the preantepenult (*calculation* 39 per cent). While there was extensive variability among individuals, Fuchs and Maxwell did not find that differences conformed to any L1 group. They also observed that the location of primary and secondary stresses were limited to the same syllables; that is, speakers might differ in whether they placed primary stress on the first or third syllables, but none stressed the second, similar to the observations in Pandey (2015).

Figure 13 provides two tokens of the word "defect," segmented from sentence contexts which made its grammatical category as a noun or verb clear; both are stressed word-finally. In the spectrogram, pitch is indicated by the lower, darker line, and intensity by the higher, thinner one. The patterns of pitch, intensity, and duration in noun and verb are nearly identical, illustrating that stress characteristics are not used to differentiate the lexical categories.

5.1.2 Acoustics of Stress

The phonetics of stress also provide common features across IndE (Pickering & Wiltshire 2000, Wiltshire & Moon 2003). Wiltshire and Moon (2003) found IndE speakers use similar cues for stress, namely, increases in pitch (F0), loudness

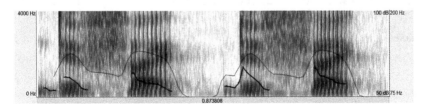

Figure 13 "Defect" as a noun vs. verb (Shillong-Khasi)
Sound 13 Audio file available at www.cambridge.org/wiltshire

(amplitude), and length (duration), and confirmed statistically that these acoustic features did not differ among five speakers each of four L1s from Indo-Aryan (Hindi, Gujarati) and Dravidian (Tamil, Telugu) groups; the shared IndE implementation of stress also significantly differs from another variety, AmE. Saha and Mandal (2016, 2017) examined the English of twenty Bengali L1 speakers, and found a similar combination of duration, intensity, and F0 differences marked the stressed syllable; again the cues were weaker than those of other English varieties. Fuchs and Maxwell (2015) examined the acoustics of both primary and secondary stress produced by their eight speakers from Hindi and Malayalam L1 backgrounds, and focusing on longer noun-verb pairs, as mentioned previously. They found that speakers produced differences in intensity, spectral balance, duration, and pitch slope that distinguished primary and secondary stress, although some cues were only significant in left-prominent words (intensity) and others only in right-prominent nouns (pitch slope). Their work also confirms that the acoustic realization of the distinction between primary/secondary stress differs from other varieties of English, but not based on L1 background.

The acoustic characteristics of stress in the L1s require further research to evaluate any role in contributing toward the IndE accent. Research thus far suggests that stress in Indian languages is often either not phonemic and/or is realized primarily by pitch, with only weak cues of intensity and duration. For example, Hindi stress has been described as not contrastive (Ohala 1999), and Dyrud (2001) and Nair (2001) both found lowered pitch on stressed syllables, with some increased syllable duration; for Tamil, Keane (2006) argues that the prominent syllable serves only as an abstract anchor for pitch accent. Furthermore, the location of stress is known to differ widely across L1s; for example, the default position for stress is final in Hindi but initial in Bengali and Telugu (Payne & Maxwell 2018). The location of stress in BrE and AmE is somewhat arbitrary and complex, and it may be that in the process of acquisition and koineization, regularization has occurred; if their L1 lacks a system of phonemic stress, IndE learners may first acquire an unmarked system, and when learners hear variable input, as in contact situations involving mixed dialects, they may regularize to new patterns (Sirsa & Redford 2013). The pattern in IndE resembles other contact varieties of English which have regularized English stress, as Peng and Ann (2001) found in three varieties: Nigerian English, Singapore English, and the English of Spanish L1 speakers. All exhibited regularities, including the tendency to stress long vowels and diphthongs, independent of L1 patterns. This tendency is likely less marked, as phonologists agree that stressed vowels prefer to be long and long vowels prefer to be stressed (e.g., Prince 1990). The placement of stress on the same syllable of a base despite suffixation has also been treated as desirable in phonological analyses, providing uniformity within a paradigm (e.g., Steriade 2000).

5.2 Intonation

Intonation uses pitch variation for grammatical roles, such as marking phrase boundaries or distinguishing questions from statements, and for extra-grammatical roles, as in conveying attitudes, connotations, or emotions. The intonation patterns used by IndE speakers have been cited as causes of misin-terpretations of discourse functions or affect in interactions with speakers of other varieties (Gumperz 1982, Kachru 1983, Pickering 1999), indicating that the pattern is distinct. Intonation also conveys information about dialect or L2 status (e.g., Van Els & De Bot 1987). Initial descriptions of IndE intonation focused on differences from BrE and from various Indian languages (CIEFL 1972, Latha 1978, Ravisankar 1994, Nair 1996), and acoustic research on the intonation of IndE is relatively in its infancy. I group it here into two main categories: overall use of pitch (mean pitch, pitch range, and dynamism), and accent and phrasing (type/function, phonetic realization, and placement).

5.2.1 Overall Use of Pitch

From studies of mean pitch and pitch dynamism/variation, it seems that speakers alter their pitch when speaking IndE compared with their L1s, although it is yet unclear how. Krishna, Krishnan, and Mittal (2018) examined productions in English and their L1s by twenty speakers each of Kannada, Telugu, and Tamil, and found raised mean value of pitch and increased pitch variation in IndE compared with the L1s. By contrast, Maxwell, Payne, and Billington (2018) generally found values in the opposite direction for their study using two speakers each of Hindi, Bengali, Tamil, and Telugu; that is, speakers tended to use lower pitch and less variability in IndE than in their L1s, although there was a great deal of variability in their small sample. The different results may also be due to the types of speakers or the task. Krishna et al. (2018) specify that they excluded English teaching faculty and the "convent educated," and their speakers read texts including technical literature, while Maxwell et al. (2018) specify their subjects as university students who began learning English early (ages four to seven), who read the "North wind and the sun" passage as if narrating a story. In both cases, however, speakers change their prosodic behavior when using IndE, a result that requires further investigation.

Fuchs (2018) evaluates a range of pitch features of both read and spontaneous speech produced in English from twenty speakers of IndE, five each of L1 Bengali, Hindi, Malayalam, and Telugu. He finds no significant differences based on L1 group for measures of mean and median pitch, skewness of the F0, pitch range, and pitch dynamism quotient, indicating some homogeneity in their IndE. Fuchs does not compare the speakers' IndE to their L1s, but instead to BrE, finding that IndE speakers tend to speak at a higher pitch and use a wider range in spontaneous speech, while, as Fuchs (2018: 893) notes, "learners commonly have a compressed pitch range compared to native speakers." Thus, the behavior of his IndE speakers does not resemble learner varieties, and the comparisons of four L1 backgrounds suggests homogeneity in their IndE use of pitch.

5.2.2 Pitch Accent and Phrasing

For pitch accent, IndE appears to have developed a distinct system that applies multiple accents per intonational phrase; the choice of which accents varies across IndE varieties. Wiltshire and Harnsberger's (2006) comparison of IndE produced by L1 Tamil and Gujarati speakers found commonality in that both groups assign pitch accents to most or all of the content words before the intonational phrase boundary, but "[Gujarati English] speakers typically use a rising pitch accent transcribed here as LH, while [Tamil English] speakers use either a falling pitch accent (HL), a high pitch accent (H), or a rising pitch accent (LH)" (Wiltshire & Harnsberger 2006: 101). Tamil speakers used significantly more falling HL, while Gujarati speakers used significantly more rising LH, than did the other group.

Moon (2002) also suggested a difference in the pitch accents used for focus in Hindi vs. Telugu L1 speakers, based on his investigation of the phonetic cues to focus in IndE compared with AmE. Using read data from three Hindi and four Telugu L1 speakers, he measured the three main phonetic cues to focus prominence: amplitude/loudness, duration/length, and F0/pitch. For amplitude, the Telugu group showed a greater increase on focused syllables than unfocused, compared with the Hindi group or AmE groups, while for duration, both IndE groups did not use lengthening for focus, unlike his AmE speakers. For pitch, he found that all groups had similar maximum pitches on the focused syllable, but there were differences in where the maximum was realized and the shape of the contour in the focused syllable. The Hindi group lowered F0 more at the beginning, followed by a sharper rise compared with the Telugu group; to represent this phonologically, Moon suggested different focus accents: L+H* for Hindi speakers and H* for the Telugu speakers, where a plus sign (+) indicates an accent that is bitonal and the asterisk (*) indicates which tone is aligned with stress.

Pitch accent and focus are also examined in Puri (2013), who compares intonation in the IndE of simultaneous vs. late Hindi-English bilinguals in

Delhi, aged nineteen to thirty-four, and finds differences depending on age of acquisition. Her twenty simultaneous bilinguals began their acquisition of both English and Hindi at home before age three, though no details were provided on how much later the ten "late" bilinguals began learning English. Puri examined pitch accent type and focus accent realizations in both groups reading sentences in both IndE and Hindi. She reports that in declarative sentences, both groups marked every non-final content word with a pitch accent in both Hindi and IndE, and both groups used an LH pitch accent in both languages; this was the only accent type used in Hindi. The simultaneous bilinguals, however, used two additional pitch accents in their IndE, H* and H*+L. However, five speakers from this group were responsible for most of the non-LH accents, and, because all five had attended convent schools, type of education as well as age of acquisition may be a factor.

Puri also found differences in the phonetic realizations of focused and post-focus syllables between the two groups, both in Hindi and IndE. While both groups marked the focused syllable with longer duration, bigger pitch excursions, and greater amplitude than post-focus syllables in both languages, they differed in their use of duration in IndE; the late bilinguals had greater durational differences between focused and post-focus syllables in IndE. Puri suggests that the "age of acquisition of a New English can be one of the factors that contribute in the variation found in the variety" (Puri 2013: 117). Thus while Sirsa and Redford (2013) found that speakers of different L1s may produce similar IndE features, Puri has shown that speakers of the same L1 may produce IndE differently, depending on age of acquisition and probably type of education.

Maxwell (2014) examined both the phonetic and phonological systems of intonation among a different kind of population: eight L1 speakers of Bengali and Kannada who, unlike other studies here, were all older (aged forty to fifty) medical professionals; also unusually, some had lived in Australia for years (ranging from three to fourteen years). Maxwell used both read and spontaneous speech, and detected differences among her speakers sometimes attributable to their L1 groups. For example, Maxwell (2014: 240) determined that the accentual density noted in Wiltshire and Harnsberger (2006) and Puri (2013) is not uniform; L1 Kannada speakers had a higher density than L1 Bengali speakers. Maxwell did find similarities as well among the IndE speakers; duration, F0 height and excursion, and RMS amplitude were all used to mark prominence in the realization of focus, though, as with stress, vowel quality was marginal, at best. She also found boundary lengthening in both groups, differentiating between the intermediate phrase and intonational phrases, although the Bengali group lengthened more phrase-finally than did the Kannada group. In terms of phrase accents, the groups also share the same types of phrase accents (H-, L-, and !H-, where the exclamation point indicates a downstepped or relatively lowered H) and boundary tones (H% and L%), but, as in Wiltshire and Harnsberger (2006), the pitch accent inventories differed; both included H*, L*, L+H* and !H*, but Bengali speakers had additional accents (L*+H, L+!H*, L*+!H).

The Bengali speakers' use of the L*+H accent also found in Bengali (Hayes & Lahiri 1991) seems a good candidate for L1 influence on intonation. Maxwell makes a convincing case that that L1 is not the only factor, nor does IndE differ from other Englishes merely because it is generally learned as an L2: "The fact that the highly educated and fluent speakers in this study still placed accents on more words and at times grouped utterances into more phrases . . . indicate that these features could be part of IndE intonational phonology" (Maxwell 2014: 245). Overall, Maxwell found widespread commonalities that provide IndE with its unique character, while also sharing similarities with well-established Englishes, including phrasing (prosodic constituency) and tune/boundary tone inventories. On the other hand, Maxwell's findings show variation in accentual density, pitch accent inventory, and choice of pitch accent in focus, for her two groups of speakers.

Further variability may be found in the intonational character of northeast IndE accents, especially those of speakers of Tibeto-Burman tonal languages, an area on which there is yet no phonetic research. Wiltshire (2005) observed informally that pitch variation seemed restrained in Tibeto-Burman IndE, with fewer pitch accents than other varieties of IndE. Similarly, Lalrindiki (1989) observed that Mizo speakers may be perceived as "flat" or "toneless" in their English, and suggested "that Mizo speakers consider the pitch system of Mizo and English to be so different that the former should not be allowed to influence the latter at all and hence the tonelessness of the latter" (1989: 29).

Figure 14 presents a sentence from a reading passage produced by the Shillong-Khasi speaker.[8] Although Shillong is in northeast India, Khasi is not a tone language. In the spectrogram, the sentence "and so the North wind was obliged to confess that the sun was the stronger of the two" appears to contain four pitch accents as shown by the pitch line, illustrating some accentual density.

For sources of intonation, the pool of features during the development of IndE includes those of the substrate languages at the time. The increased density of accents in IndE may be related to a similar pattern seen in current Indian

---

[8] His reading of the entire passage, and that of the Mumbai-Marathi speaker, are available in the supplementary resources on-line.

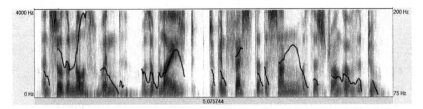

Figure 14 Sentence from "The north wind and sun" passage, Shillong-Khasi speaker

Sound 14 Audio file available at www.cambridge.org/wiltshire

languages, including Bengali (Hayes & Lahiri 1991, Khan 2014), Hindi (Rajendran & Yegnanarayana 1996, Patil et al. 2008), and Tamil (Keane 2014); research in each shows a tendency for every (non-final) prosodic word to act as an accentual phrase and take a pitch accent of its own. However, works on the current intonation of Indian languages seems primarily focused on these three, while research on the whole range of languages or their antecedents is not sufficiently nor uniformly developed. Normally, we should also look to the intonational systems of the dialects of English present during the formative years, but documentation of those systems is likewise insufficient. Certainly differences exist within Englishes in Great Britain now: "Experimental research on the inventory and distribution of pitch accents in BrE has shown the preference for a rising pitch on accented words in Glasgow English and some varieties of Irish English as well as a smaller inventory of pitch accents," writes Maxwell (2014: 20), suggesting that the feature pool contained options that may be reflected today.

5.3 Rhythm

The rhythm of a language is often considered its most distinctive feature, and IndE's rhythm has generally been described as syllable-timed (CIEFL 1972, Wells 1982, Bansal 1983, Kachru 1983), in which each syllable has equal duration. Syllable-timing contrasts with stress-timing, in which stressed syllables are longer than unstressed, giving feet roughly equal duration. However, the original formulation of these terms has been challenged (Roach 1982, Dauer 1983), and current research explores a continuum of rhythmic options rather than a dichotomy, based on acoustic measures that characterize various rhythmic properties. Measures include %V, the percentage of duration in an utterance that is vocalic (Ramus et al. 1999), higher in languages perceived as syllable-timed because they tend to lack vowel reduction and have fewer consonant clusters. A second common measure is nPVI, or normalized Pairwise Variability Index (Grabe & Low 2002), which compares the duration of each vowel to an adjacent vowel, providing a measure that reflects the degree of variability across an utterance and is normally lower in syllable-timed languages. The perception of rhythm is considered to result from a combination of such factors. Though both the terminology "syllable-/stress-timing" and individual measures of rhythm have limitations as well (e.g., Arvaniti 2009), the results in the following are discussed using the terminology and metrics provided by each study.

Two recent studies have evaluated rhythm measures on IndE: Fuchs (2013) and Sirsa and Redford (2013). Fuchs (2013) provides more measures of IndE and a direct comparison to BrE using comparable methods; however, he does not evaluate whether there is variation within IndE. In addition to measures that focus on duration, he examines correlates of prominence such as variability in loudness and pitch, based on twenty speakers of IndE from four language groups: Bengali, Hindi, Malayalam, and Telugu, compared with data from ten speakers of BrE. Overall, he found the IndE speech to be more syllable-timed in having less variability of vocalic durations, a higher percentage of voiced duration per utterance, and less variability in intensity than BrE. He also found that prominence in IndE was less cued by loudness and duration, as noted in the discussion of stress (Section 5.1.2); this contributes to a "syllable-timing" percept as the various units of speech (syllable, foot) differ less from each other than in stress-timed BrE. The only correlate that IndE shares with more stress-timed languages is a lower speech rate. Overall, Fuchs considers rhythmic factors a commonality in the emerging standard for educated speakers, regardless of their origin or L1, but he did not directly test that claim.

Sirsa and Redford (2013) do test it, by evaluating rhythmic characteristics of the IndE and L1s of speakers of Hindi and Telugu (seven each), and conclude that "the analyses on global rhythm metrics and speech rate suggested that IE has a rhythm pattern that is distinct from either Hindi or Telugu, and that the native language has little influence on speakers' production of IE rhythm" (2013: 402). They measured %V, nPVI, ΔC (standard deviation of consonant duration), and speech rate, and found no significant difference on any measures in the IndE of the two groups, though there were differences between the L1s. Sirsa and Redford found only one difference in duration, namely that Hindi L1 speakers lengthen more phrase-finally in Hindi and IndE than Telugu speakers do. Their measured value for %V in IndE (46.8 per cent) was lower than in both the L1s (Hindi 52.3 per cent/Telugu 51.2 per cent), while for ΔC IndE's value (29.7 per cent) was higher (Hindi 28.6 per cent / Telugu 26.4 per cent), indicating the speakers change their rhythm in IndE and move toward more stress-timing than the L1s. These measures can also tentatively be compared with results reported elsewhere for BrE: IndE's %V (46.8 per cent) is well above Grabe and Low's (2002) measure for BrE (41.1 per cent), while the IndE ΔC (29.7) is well below Ramus et al.'s (1999) ΔC for BrE (54 per cent), both indicating more syllable-timing. Their study directly supports the uniformity of an IndE rhythm that is not identical to that of the two L1s, nor like BrE.

Finally, Payne and Maxwell (2018) investigate some further measures of durational variability that may contribute to rhythm, and find evidence both of L1 influence and shared temporal characteristics across IndE. Their eight IndE speakers came from four L1 backgrounds (Hindi, Bengali, Tamil, Telugu), and Payne and Maxwell measured durational contrasts of tense/lax vowels, stressed/ unstressed, and phrase-final/medial position. In addition to finding length differences for the tense/lax contrast for all groups except Bengali (mentioned in Section 4.2.5), Payne and Maxwell did find stress-conditioned lengthening for all speakers in most positions, with the Bengali and Tamil speakers lengthening in all positions, but both Hindi and Telugu not lengthening finally. For phrase-final lengthening, where Sirsa and Redford (2013) found greater lengthening in Hindi L1 & IndE than Telugu L1 & IndE, Payne and Maxwell (2018) found that unstressed vowels lengthen finally, but stressed vowels generally did not, except for one L1 Bengali speaker. Phrase-final lengthening of unstressed syllables and lack of lengthening in stressed syllables shortens the durational difference between syllable types. Further lengthening of stressed syllables that were already long, Payne & Maxwell suggest, might be avoided in order limit variability for a more syllable-timed rhythm. They also suggest that resistance to additive lengthening is a possible 'pan-Indian English' feature.

Kachru (1983) explicitly attributes the rhythm of IndE to transfer: "the underlying reasons for the deviations in stress are the following: all the main SALs [=South Asian Languages] are syllable-timed languages, as opposed to English, which is a stress-timed language" (1983: 31). Even if transfer were the source of rhythm, however, IndE would likely not be monolithic, as not all languages in India resemble each other. Sirsa and Redford (2013), for example, showed that Hindi and Telugu differed on durational features while the IndE of these speakers did not, apart from phrase-final lengthening, so that shared norms rather than transfer provided a better explanation. As with intonation, it is difficult to determine the rhythmic characteristics of L1s and English varieties hundreds of years ago, but we can again observe that BrE currently has varieties with similar features to IndE. For example, informally, a British novelist describes an Indian immigrant in England thus: "In her voice were hints of the singsong tone, Welsh in its rhythms, so characteristic of the Indian speaking

English" (Rendell 1987: 17), while more empirically, Fuchs (2013) writes that "results on British dialects (such as Ferragne 2008) showed that some dialects spoken in the British Isles are likely to be as syllable-timed as educated IndE. These dialects might have at least contributed to a tendency toward syllable-timing in educated IndE" (2013: 190).

5.4 Suprasegmental Overview for Uniformity vs. Variability

I have examined stress, intonation, and rhythm, which involve phonetic characteristics of intensity, pitch, and duration. The location of stress and its acoustic realizations are shared widely, though individual and possibly local variations exist for both. For pitch, altered pitch and pitch range seem to characterize IndE, while for intonational units, there is a tendency to place pitch accents on more words, though which accents vary in different groups (Wiltshire & Harnsberger 2006, Maxwell 2014). IndE is more syllable-timed than BrE on a variety of measures (Fuchs 2013) and speakers tend to share rhythmic features in IndE despite having divergent features in their L1s (Sirsa & Redford 2013). IndE is in fact so stereotypically perceived to be syllable-timed that when Fuchs (2015) manipulated samples through resynthesis to make them completely isochronous and played them to British and Indian listeners, both sets of listeners rated such samples as more Indian than real unmanipulated IndE samples.

Table 11 Overview for suprasegmentals

Widespread uniformity	Variability
Stress location based on syllable weight	Individual variation
Acoustic features of stress	Use of length (Bengali)
Altered pitch range/variability	Direction of alteration
Multiple pitch accents per phrase	Extent of accentual density
Overlapping inventory of pitch accents	Complete inventory and which pitch accents used more, realization of focus accent
Intonational phrasing, phrase accents and boundary tones	
Boundary lengthening	Extent of lengthening
Rhythmic measures tend toward syllable timing	

The overall picture from suprasegmentals (Table 11), as with consonants and vowels, reveals a core of commonalities shared across IndE, with local and L1 differences when we examine most of these characteristics more closely.

6 Variation: Perception(s) and Attitudes

Research on attitudes toward English in India tends to show increasing acceptance of IndE, especially as appropriate for use within the country (Section 2.2). IndE speakers also generally feel that they can perceive differences within IndE accents. Research on whether they have that ability is scarce but tends to support their intuitions, while computational approaches support the feasibility of distinguishing among IndE accents (Section 6.1). Attitudes toward this variation, as evidenced by comments from IndE speakers and by their behavior leads to a discussion of the role of IndE accents in identity expression (Section 6.2).

6.1 Ability to Perceive Variation within IndE

Jawaharlal Nehru is quoted as saying, in 1963, "We have arrived at a stage where people talk about Punjabi English, Bengali English, Madrasi English and so forth. They say that every part of India has its own brand of English in the way of pronunciation and so on and it is undoubtedly so" (Nagarajan 1985: 6). Nehru may have meant geographic variation ("Madrasi") instead of or in addition to L1 based variation (Bengali and Punjabi both being ambiguous); in any case, the quote indicates that Indian users of English have long perceived variation within IndE. A similar comment specifically about IndE accent comes from Shastri (1992: 263), who observes "[t]he moment an Indian opens his mouth he announces himself as not only an Indian but perhaps as a Madrasi, Gujarati, Punjabi, and so on." However, Shastri also qualifies this description as true only for average Indians, as opposed to English-medium educated speakers who are near-native/native and speak more than one subvariety, adjusting their accents to their audiences. He thus implies control in registers as well as subvarieties for advanced speakers of IndE, and the ability to control production as well as to perceive variation.

Kachru's survey, described in Section 2.2, explicitly asked IndE speakers how many varieties of IndE they recognized, and although about a sixth of respondents reported only one, more reported two (17.7 per cent) and three (16.7 per cent), with another 33.1 per cent saying between four and ten (Kachru 1976: 233–4). I have found little further reported on IndE speakers' sense of whether they can distinguish among varieties within India, so in gathering data from Assamese speakers in October 2019, we asked "Can you tell from someone's accent in English where they're from?" and seventeen of twenty-four reported that they could. Those who answered negatively sometimes said, "I can't," which might be a comment on their abilities rather than the possibility more theoretically. Popular culture also reflects this sense that different IndE varieties exist, evidenced, for example, in comic online videos, performed by speakers of IndE exaggerating and parodying accent differences from different regions/L1s. Another video also reflects pride in IndE accents, presenting public figures from different origins with the stated goal "to counteract the stereotype that all Indians sound like Apu on the Simpsons."[9]

While IndE speakers may feel that they can identify variations within IndE, Sridhar (1989), referring to Kachru's survey, pointed out that "the accuracy and reliability of such identifications, however, have yet to be researched" (1989: 43). To a large extent this remains true; however, a few studies show IndE speakers distinguishing among speakers from different L1 and geographic groups, such Sirsa and Redford (2013), Sitaram et al. (2018), and Chakraborty and Didla (2020). Computational analyses also demonstrate that distinguishing varieties based on L1 is possible for automatic systems (Imani et al. 2019, Krishna & Krishnan 2014), that performance improves when IndE models are used (Joshi & Rao 2013, Phull & Kumar 2016), and that such analyses can suggest which acoustic features to investigate for their effects on humans' perception of variation (Krishna & Krishnan 2017).

Sirsa and Redford (2013), who acoustically analyzed the production of IndE and the L1s of seven speakers each of Hindi and Telugu, also created a perceptual judgment task for nine naïve L1 AmE speakers and ten experienced listeners, who were Hindi and Telugu L1 speakers living in the USA. Listeners heard IndE samples of two different sentences produced by two different IndE speakers; naïve listeners also heard the L1 versions of the same sentences. In half the trials, speakers came from the same L1 background; in the other half, they came from different L1 groups. Listeners were told that the speech samples would come from native Hindi and native Telugu speakers, and to judge whether speakers had the same or different background. Although naïve listeners easily distinguished between the L1 samples, they were less reliable at distinguishing the IndE of the two groups; experienced listeners, however, accurately discriminated between the IndE of Hindi and Telugu L1 speakers. Thus the differences between IndE varieties are more subtle than the differences between the L1s, reinforcing Sirsa and Redford's general hypothesis of convergence to IndE norms away from features of individual L1s, but the IndE of different L1s can be distinguished, at least by experienced listeners such as speakers of those varieties.

[9] Parodies: www.youtube.com/watch?v=-hEXj9AqmvE, https://www.youtube.com/watch?v=1PgEwZI76Ho Pride: www.youtube.com/watch?v=v9arM_agKFA&list=PLYPtb9q4_WuR2pbEh ZWTbhfKHNpPACOyE

The field of automatic speech recognition (ASR) seems to have accepted variation within IndE as given. Sitaram et al. (2018) argue that better training data is needed to improve ASR systems to deal with IndE variation and, in the absence of sufficient research on the acoustic characteristics of varieties or corpora labelled with detailed demographic information on their speakers, they investigate a crowdsourcing approach. This involves playing audio samples from IndE speakers and asking users to identify where the speaker comes from. Ideally, a consensus from the users would enable the identification of a set of candidate accents, as well as indicating which accents are most distinct or confusable. Unfortunately, the only demographic information for their data was the location where it was collected, which they treat as the origins of their speakers. The sixty listeners were often able to place a label on the regions "South Indian" and "North Indian" in agreement with the geographical information, suggesting that these might be major dialectal zones. Listeners were not as successful on the other three zone choices: North East, Central, Middle East, possibly because these are not distinct zones or because the geographic data did not reflect the true origins of the speakers. Sitaram et al. also asked each of the sixty listeners to provide a sample of their own speech along with demographic background data, to a web app-based study with better labeled data. A pilot testing of this app with ten users resulted in fairly low scores (40/100), and "users pointed out that the accents were difficult to guess because the speakers were very urban with mild accents" (Sitaram et al. 2018: 2880). Thus while some speakers can be placed into their general accent area by other speakers in India, other accents, described as mild and urban, are more difficult to distinguish.

Finally, Chakraborty and Didla (2020) performed a small-scale perceptual study to test whether ten naïve listeners could categorize twelve speakers of IndE from known geographic backgrounds which they divided into six "zones" (North, North East, East, West, Central, and South). Both speakers and listeners were in their twenties to early thirties and were students or faculty at EFLU in Hyderabad. Speakers read the Rainbow passage, and the listeners, also from diverse states of India, were asked to guess which of the six zones the speaker was from. The results suggested that speakers from the South were most easily identified (95 per cent), followed by speakers from the Northeast (80 per cent). While results from the other options were not as good, ranging from 35–70 per cent accurate categorization, they are far above chance and may be significant, though no statistics were provided, likely because the samples were small. Furthermore, the failure to better categorize speakers into other "zones" may again indicate only that the options the researchers provided do not match actual or perceived dialect groups. One "misidentification" they cite as common was that the speaker from Assam, included in their "East" dialect with the Bengali speaker, was classified by listeners as Northeast, a category which included one speaker each from Nagaland and Mizoram. While Assamese and Bengali share a family history as eastern branch members of Indo-Aryan (Masica 1991), the categorization of a speaker from Assam with the Northeast speakers more closely reflects the geographic and political affiliation of Assam, and may not be a misidentification at all. Overall, research tends to confirm IndE speakers' ability to distinguish speakers' dialect origins based on accent features, though larger studies need to be conducted to determine the extent and limitations, as well as the basis, of this capacity.

Other approaches to identifying L1s based on variation within the IndE accents are completely computer-based, and these have proven quite successful at distinguishing even among samples from speakers of closely related L1s which share phonological characteristics. Imani et al. (2019) used data from speakers from Northeast/East India: thirty-five Assamese, thirty-three Bengali, and thirty Bodo speakers reading English, and found that their language identification system reached an accuracy of 59 per cent using samples as short as 3 seconds, even though they did not use any features of pitch in the analysis. However, we lack any information about the speakers' level of education or English proficiency. Krishna and Krishnan (2014) use both segmental and prosodic characteristics of the English spoken by native speakers of Telugu, Tamil, and Kannada, all Dravidian languages of South India, and their language identification modelling reached 80–85 per cent accuracies in categorization. In this study, their speakers are described as educated to graduation and fluent in English, but they did explicitly exclude English teachers and the convent educated. Krishna and Krishnan (2017) investigate the same groups but also provide more detail into which features are most useful in distinguishing varieties. Often these are quite specific, such as the highest pitch variations (maximum–minimum) during the velar nasal for Telugu L1 speakers, or the lowest pitch variations for the rhotics of Tamil speakers. Not only does this show that finding such characteristics is possible using computational methods, but also it may provide clues about what differences are present that human listeners may also be able to use, which can suggest further perceptual studies.

Computational research has also shown that ASR systems perform better on IndE speech when trained on IndE databases. For example, Joshi and Rao (2013) assess the English vowels produced by Gujarati L1 speakers, who were chosen because of their clearly accented speech in English and their Gujarati-medium education. They found improvement in the performance of their ASR model in recognizing vowels by creating and using a "General Indian English" database of model speakers who they consider to lack any specifically recognizable accent, instead of existing non-IndE databases. Phull and Kumar (2016) performed ASR on lectures given by speakers of IndE from a variety of backgrounds, and compared their results based on whether the system was trained with British, American, or Indian speech samples. Their measures of Word Error Rate (WER) were better using an IndE model (31 per cent compared with 38 per cent average error rate for other models), although they noted that the model they developed was based on South Indian speakers only and performed better on South than North Indian speakers. Phull and Kumar suggest that further performance improvements could be made with better models for varieties of IndE, stating a need "to "deal with the discrepancies between variants of IndE accents by building pronunciation models for different accents" (2016: 4173).

Thus, speakers' attitudes, performances on perceptual tests, and computational approaches all support the claim of variation within IndE accents, and further research in these areas may suggest features that distinguish them.

6.2 Attitudes toward Variation within IndE

As with the ability to perceive differences within IndE, the attitude toward such differences needs further study. How users of English in India feel about variation in IndE accents can be evaluated directly, in experiments and interview questions, and indirectly, by behavioral observations. As an example of the former, Bansal (1990: 230) summarizes an early unpublished MLitt thesis from CIEFL that compared reactions to varieties: "Ramunny (1976) investigated the subjective reactions of a cross-section of Indian society to some of the varieties of English speech commonly found in the country. The two supra-regional speakers emerged clearly above the five regional speakers on the basis of the preferences indicated by 106 respondents representing a wide range of occupations." As an example of the latter, speakers' behavior can indirectly reveal their evaluation of a feature; sociolinguistic studies that collect data in more than one style can reveal the relative prestige attached to features based on their use. For example, Domange (2011) found that his high-use IndE speakers used more interdental fricatives in more formal styles, suggesting that these speakers were able to manipulate it as a sociolinguistically prestigious feature. Furthermore, the lack of register sensitivity can indicate neutrality or acceptance as part of a standard IndE, as in the case of [ʋ/w] use, which Sahgal and Agnihotri (1988: 100) reported as not changing in formal vs. casual speech. These two studies were both based in Delhi, and wider research is needed to determine the variability of attitudes toward specific features through sociolinguistic behavior.

Apart from the Ramunny (1976) thesis previously mentioned, interviews and surveys tend to ask only about attitudes toward IndE or its accent in general, but they have also elicited comments relevant to variation. Sharma (2005) found that her speakers, IndE speakers living in the USA, consider accents separately from grammar, with a less prescriptive attitude toward variation in accents. For example, one speaker agrees that the IndE accent is different from the AmE, but that "it's up to you . . . It doesn't matter, it doesn't, I mean, categorize you in some way. It's just your accent and the way you speak" (Sharma 2005: 216). Chand (2009) found a similar freedom from prescriptive attitudes about accent in the sociolinguistic interviews she conducted with upper-middle-class Hindi/ English bilinguals in South Delhi. Some speakers describe IndE as the neutral variety, with no accent, especially in local use, while varieties such as AmE are said to have accents (or "a twang"). One speaker describes IndE as more accepting of variability in accents, saying that in contrast to the British, who make judgments based on pronunciations, IndE is "a little bit more liberal. It's a little bit more open" (Chand 2009: 410). Fuchs (2015: 125) asked Indian users of English whether they preferred hearing a certain accent, and reported that the "[a]nswers to these questions were almost unanimous . . . the main requirement that informants gave was that whatever accent a speaker may use, it should be intelligible. This indicates a great tolerance towards accents other than their own."

Both Chand (2009) and Fuchs (2015) also elicited comments on the use of "fake accents." Chand (2009) elicits stories and comments about people who have adopted different accents after short trips abroad, and her participants generally disapprove of such behavior. One remarks, "You can be a social embarrassment if you do that. We will embarrass you." (Chand 2009: 412). As Chand points out, such an interaction "illuminates IE's local social value. Youths who use fake accents are interpreted as being embarrassed by their heritage and nation, and IE is taken up as a symbol of national pride and linguistic confidence." Fuchs (2015) also asked his participants how they would feel toward a speaker who grew up in India and adopted a British or American accent, and finds a similar intolerance, although in addition to calling them "fake," informants were also convinced that IndE speakers could not succeed in reproducing foreign accents. Fuchs quotes one as saying "[t]hey speak with their polished British/American accent, but at some point their Bangla/Telugu/Hindi etc. accent resurfaces" (2015: 125), revealing not only the attitude toward adopting an external accent, but again a recognition of variation within IndE accents. IndE speakers thus express evaluations of their own accents through their negative judgments of speakers who emulate external norms like BrE or AmE.

The reaction to the use of non-local accents as inauthentic leads to the issue of identity as expressed through language in general and accent in particular. Language is used to express not only content but also social meanings including identity, whether as a member of one group or as distinct from other groups, and language's "role as an identity-marker may be more powerful than its role as a means of communication" (Agnihotri & Khanna 1997: 12). Is an identity expressed through an IndE accent generally or through variations within IndE accents? The question also requires addressing the issue of whether there is a general Indian identity, only a more local identity, or both. It is possible that the IndE accent does not particularly carry an identity for its users. As Schneider (2007) points out, the primary motivations for acquiring English are instrumental so that perhaps "a local form of English has not adopted the function of an identity-carrier" and instead, speakers "will use English for certain purposes but their identity remains rooted in their cultural heritage" (2007: 167). Speakers' nonjudgmental attitudes about accents also support the position that there is no strong identity associated with accent features.

On the other hand, IndE and its variations may have become useful as an identity-carrier which, along with other Indian L1s, is used to express ties to local cultures. Author Neelum Saran Gour (2010) who describes herself as having written in several IndE varieties, writes: "What makes it Bengali-English or Urdu-English or Hindi-English? It's not a sprinkling of words alone but an activation of auditory memory in the author's and the reader's mind. It is the awakening of pictures, the resonance of living voices, speech rhythms, thought-circles, slopes of metaphor, the scent of an entire culture." (2010: 117). For her, the local accent evokes a local culture linked with a local identity. A sense of pan-Indian identity may also be growing, as Chand (2009: 405) argues "There is evidence from several corners that modern Indian urban culture(s) has/have developed: Speakers now identify as "Indian" over narrower ethnolinguistic, religious, and regional identities (Raj 2003)." Based on comments from her IndE speakers living in the USA, Sharma (2005: 217) suggests that "phonology is seen in less prescriptive terms and may be recruited more readily for the construction of a local Indian identity." In Sharma's study, the identity at issue is Indian vs. American, but the same attitude might allow for IndE internal variation to be recruited for identity within India.

I suggest that for at least some speakers, particularly highly educated, urban, well-traveled bilinguals, both local and pan-Indian identity can be expressed through their IndE accents (Sahgal & Agnihotri 1988, Mallikarjun 2020). The question of local vs. national identity in some cases depends on context. Krishnaswamy and Burde (1998) claim that "one is a Bengali or Punjabi or Tamilian while in India; only when one goes outside India, he/she becomes an 'Indian' because the outside world and the passport say so. No one in India feels h/she is an Indian" (1998: 63). Within India, identity is maintained as a member of a local community based on L1, religion, region, etc., while the identity as an Indian may emerge only in contrast to outsiders. But a pan-Indian identity growing among a subset of speakers within India may be finding its expression through English as well, though development of a national identity will not obviate the need for more local identities. Sahgal and Agnihotri (1988) describe the duality: "the pressures of urbanization involving literacy, education, mass media, westernization etc. favor the evolution of a norm; on the other hand, the different linguistic and cultural backgrounds of different groups in Delhi favor diversity, with Bengalis speaking a 'Bengali English' and Tamils speaking a 'Tamil English'" (1988: 54). The expression of identity using accent features requires some recognition that those features link with specific groups, as Eckert (2019) reasons that "[r]egional and ethnic phonological features take on idexicality based on common construals of the population in which they originated" (2019: 760), and IndE speakers sense of the phonetic and phonological attributes of IndE and subvarieties of it make its use as an expression of identity possible. Where there is a pan-Indian identity, features of IndE can be used to express it; where there are subgroup identities, variations within IndE can be used to distinguish them. Where there are differences in IndE accents that signify social differences, we would expect those characteristics to persist. In fact, Sirsa and Redford (2013) predict that "strong social and regional pressures could drive the evolution of IE into multiple varieties that would keep language-affiliated identities alive" (2013: 404).

Schneider (2007: 167) summarized that "The identity constructions of English speakers in India during the twentieth century were presumably as compartmentalized and versatile as the uses of the language were" (2007: 167) which surely will be only more true in the twenty-first century.

7 Conclusions

In Tables 4, 10 and 11, I have identified a set of core features shared across the subcontinent that can be considered part of the IndE accent, along with differences based on local or regional varieties or known sociolinguistic variation. I combine most of these findings into Table 12, which organizes them from most uniform to most variable, though the order of listing within categories is not

Table 12 Reorganizing features into categories of uniformity and variability

Most uniform

Consonants	Vowels	Suprasegmentals
Prevoiced /b d g/ vs. voiceless /p t k/ with aspiration optional	Vowel quality maintained in unstressed positions	Use of intonational phrasing, boundary tones, & multiple pitch accents per phrase
Use of dental stops [t̪ʰ] [d̪]	FACE & GOAT monophthongs	Rhythmic measures tend toward syllable timing
Use of approximant [ʋ]	LOT & THOUGHT merger	Stress location based on syllable weight alone

Widespread but with known variability

Retroflexes present (absent by region, L1, sociolinguistic factors)	Use of length & quality for contrast (lack of one or both by region, L1)	Pitch accent inventory overlaps, (realization, use & extent of density vary by L1)
Modal rhotic tap (modal approximant & frequency of others by region, L1)	NORTH VS. FORCE distinction (merged by individual, L1 & lexical)	Boundary lengthening (extent varies by L1)
Realization of contrast <v>/<w> (by region, L1)	System of diphthong contrasts (realizations vary by L1, individual, lexical)	Acoustic features of stress similar (vary by L1)
Dental fricative [θ], [ð] use (by sociolinguistic & linguistic conditioning)	Realization of the vowel in LOT /THOUGHT (regional, individual variation)	Altered pitch range & variability (direction and extent vary, unknown)

Mostly Variable

Post-vocalic rhoticity/non-rhoticity (by region, sociolinguistics)

meaningful. Type of variability, where known, is indicated in parentheses. This is meant to provide something of a snapshot of where we are now in our understanding of IndE accent features, to be changed as research progresses and as IndE develops.

Both similarities and differences, often described in terms of transfer from L1, may also or may instead be attributed to factors such as founder effects, regularization during koineization, regional pressures, and educational and orthographic systems. Often there are multiple sources of common features, as might be expected in evolutionary models of language contact, in which the frequency of a feature in the pool leads to more replications.

Why do some features tend to be uniform while others are variable? For some features, the convergence on uniformity seems inevitable, as for the monophthongs where multiple pressures (founder effects, L1s, markedness) favor the same outcome. Other features face conflicting pressures, as from different L1s, but neither the L1 nor the IndE norms always wins. For example, Tamil speakers reduce vowels in non-prominent positions in Tamil (Keane 2006) but not in their IndE (Nagarajan 1985), while Bengali speakers lack vowel length contrasts in both Bengali and in IndE (Payne & Maxwell 2018) despite most IndE speakers' use of length contrasts. Retroflexes provide an interesting example, as where they are used, they have been found to be more similar in IndE than they are in the speakers' L1s (Sirsa & Redford 2013), but on the other hand, they are also absent entirely from the northeast region, where they are also absent in the L1s (Wiltshire 2005). Why do particular features reflect L1 differences and others converge despite them? I don't know. But if IndE has formed a stable new variety from the mixture of dialects spoken around the country, then we expect dialect focusing has worked via processes of leveling, accommodation, and koineization within the speech community (Trudgill 2004). Although, in theory, a new dialect contains fewer variants than were present in all the original dialects that mixed, Britain and Trudgill (2009) argue that multiple variants can survive leveling by reallocation, where they serve a new social or linguistic function in the dialect. The use of particular rhotics, or rhoticity vs. non-rhoticity in general, may be an example of this; variants survive to be used for sociolinguistic functions. The convergence of retroflexes to a shared quality in IndE despite differences in L1 reflects koineization, while the continued lack of retroflexes in Northeast India might reflect their physical distance from the central Indian speech communities and concomitant lack of participation in the new dialect formation, or it may linguistically mark their determination to remain distinct from the central varieties. It is worth pointing out that the two more identifiable dialects in Chakraborty and

Didla (2020), the South and Northeast accents, are both regions known to value their unique cultures and to favor English over Hindi.

Yet to be considered a variety, IndE should arguably have some internal coherence and some external differences from other varieties. We could try to organize these features in terms of being necessary and/or sufficient parts of a general IndE accent. For example, the prevoicing of voiced stops and optional aspiration of voiceless stops may be a necessary feature of IndE accents, but is not sufficient to identify a speaker as using an IndE accent because it is not unique to them; the same characteristic persists in older Scottish varieties (Scobbie 2006) and in newer Englishes such as Malayasian (Shahidi & Aman 2011). Similarly for the monophthongal FACE/GOAT vowels, which may be present in all IndE varieties studied so far but are also used in BrE and AmE varieties, as well as East and West Africa, Southeast Asia and the Pacific (Schneider 2004). The use of retroflex stops may be sufficient to identify a speaker as using an IndE accent, as it seems that no other variety of English currently uses them. On the other hand, they are not necessary components of all IndE accents, varying by region and possibly sociolinguistic factors. Rhoticity or non-rhoticity is neither necessary nor sufficient, given its wide variation. We could do the same exercise with features associated with subvarieties, with the same result. If there are no features that are both necessary and sufficient to mark a speaker as speaking IndE or a variety of it, then it is possible that dialect focusing is not yet complete. However, it does seem possible to demarcate IndE and its varieties with a constellation of features, as in the top rows of Table 12. The Tibeto-Burman IndE, described as a distinct variety in Wiltshire (2005: 276) because it differs in retroflexion, postvocalic rhoticity, and use of approximant [ɹ] and a specific set of vowel contrasts, nonetheless does share in the general IndE features such as monophthongal FACE/GOAT vowels, prevoicing of stops, occasional use of [ʋ], and a regularized stress system. We must conclude that even formal educated IndE allows for variation, and that while there is a great deal of overlap, speakers feel no need to be identical in their English accents, and may even find potential for identity expression through the preservation of local features.

Because India is a vast country with a population of over a billion people who vary in every conceivable way (age, sex/gender, geographic origin, L1, religion, socioeconomic status, etc.), the possibilities of dialectal variation are manifold. This means that there are also tremendous opportunities for future research on the topic of variability, including acoustic research on more varieties of speech based not only on L1 groups but also on sociolects. Research on the ability to perceive differences within IndE, and on the basis for those abilities, may also be symbiotic with computational work to improve speech recognition, helping to improve voice-related technologies. Research on attitudes about variation can help illuminate what value IndE speakers assign to variations and the extent of its correlation with identity formation. Finally, I have not discussed research on accents in the English of Indians in the diaspora, a fruitful area for research both on dialect contact and questions of identity. For example, the volume edited by Hundt and Sharma (2014) includes investigations of phonetic and phonological features of Indo-Trinidadian speech, East African Indian migrants in Britain, and South African Indian English. If a pan-Indian identity emerges most clearly outside of India, research on the diasporic community may provide more insight into the features signaling an "Indian" accent.

Appendix
Speaker Background Information

The following speakers, designated by birthplace and L1 in the text, are used to illustrate examples, with further materials posted in the supplementary resources on-line.

Place of birth	L1	Lived in	Age	Sex	Eng-med school start	Highest degree	Other languages	Parents' languages
Chennai	Tamil	Chennai to age 23, then USA	23	M	kinder-garden	post-graduate	Hindi, Sanskrit (in school)	both: Tamil, English father: Hindi also
Mumbai	Marathi	Mumbai to age 24, then USA	29	F	pre-school	Masters	Hindi, Sanskrit (in school)	both: Marathi, English, Hindi
Mysore	Kannada	Mysore to age 24, then USA	31	M	age 10	PhD	Hindi (in school)	both: Kannada, mother: English, Hindi also
Shillong	Khasi	Shillong but 6 months in USA 3 years prior	32	M	kinder-garden	MA	Hindi (in school)	both: English, Khasi, Hindi, Jaintia
Tinsukia	Assamese	Tinsukia to age 18, then Delhi to age 30, then USA	31	M	age 4	PhD	Hindi (in school), Bengali (outside)	both: Assamese, English, Hindi

References

Agnihotri, R. K., and A. L. Khanna. 1997. *Problematizing English in India.* Delhi: Sage Publications India.

Agnihotri, R. K., and Anju Sahgal. 1985. Is Indian English retroflexed and r-full? *Indian Journal of Applied Linguistics* 11: 97–108.

Ansaldo, Umberto. 2009. The Asian typology of English. *English World-Wide* 30: 133–48. DOI:10.1075/eww.30.2.02ans

Arvaniti, Amalia. 2009. Rhythm, timing and the timing of rhythm. *Phonetica* 66: 46–63. DOI:10.1159/000208930

Awan, Shaheen N., and Carolyn L. Stine. 2011. Voice onset time in Indian English-accented speech. *Clinical Linguistics & Phonetics* 25: 998–1003. DOI:10.3109/02699206.2011.619296

Balasubramanian, T. 1972. The vowels of Tamil and English: a study in contrast. *CIEFL Bulletin* 9: 27–34.

Bamgbose, Ayo. 1998. Torn between the norms: innovations in world Englishes. *World Englishes* 17: 1–14. DOI:10.1111/1467-971X.00078

Bansal, Ram K. 1976. *The Intelligibility of Indian English.* (2nd edition). Monograph 4. Hyderabad: CIEFL.

Bansal, Ram K. 1983. *Studies in Phonetics and Spoken English.* Monograph 10. Hyderabad: CIEFL.

Bansal, Ram K. 1990. The pronunciation of English in India. In Susan Ramsaran, ed., *Studies in the Pronunciation of English.* London: Routledge, 2019–33.

Bansal, Ram K., and J. B. Harrison. 2013 [1972 originally]. *Spoken English: A Manual of Speech and Phonetics.* (4th edition). Hyderabad: Orient Blackswan.

Barpujari, H. K. 1986. *The American Missionaries and North-East India (1836–1900 A.D.).* Guwahati: Spectrum Publications.

Barron, A. W. J. 1961. The English dental fricatives in India. *CIEFL Bulletin (CIEFL)* 1: 84–6.

Beckman, Jill, Michael Jessen, and Catherine Ringen. 2013. Empirical evidence for laryngeal features: aspirating vs. true voice languages. *Journal of Linguistics* 49: 259–84. DOI:10.1017/S0022226712000424

Beal, Joan. 2004. English dialects in the North of England: phonology. In Edgar Schneider, Kate Burridge, Bernd Kortmann, Rajend Mesthrie, and Clive Upton, eds., *Varieties of English.* Berlin, New York: Mouton de Gruyter, 113–33.

Bernaisch, Tobias, and Christopher Koch. 2016. Attitudes toward Englishes in India. *World Englishes* 35: 118–32. DOI:10.1111/weng.12174

Broselow, Ellen, Su-i Chen, and Chilin Wang. 1998. The emergence of the unmarked in second language phonology. *Studies in Second Language Acquisition* 20: 261–80. DOI:10.1017/S0272263198002071

Britain, David, and Peter Trudgill. 2009. New dialect formation and contact-induced reallocation: three case studies from the English fens. *International Journal of English Studies* 5: 183–209. https://revistas.um.es /ijes/article/view/47951

Bush, Clara N. 1967. Some acoustic parameters of speech and their relationships to the perception of dialect differences. *TESOL Quarterly* 1: 20–30. DOI: 10.2307/3586196

CIEFL. 1972. *The Sound System of Indian English*. Monograph 7. Hyderabad: CIEFL.

Chakraborty, Sinjini, and Grace Suneetha Didla. 2020. A forensic phonetic study of Indian English: phonetic features as an indexical marker. *International Journal of English Literature and Social Sciences* 5: 714–20. DOI: 10.22161/ijels.53.24

Chand, Vineeta. 2009. [v] at is going on? Local and global ideologies about Indian English. *Language in Society* 38: 393–419. DOI:10.1017/ S0047404509990200

Chand, Vineeta. 2010. Postvocalic (r) in urban Indian English. *English World-Wide* 31: 1–39. DOI:10.1075/eww.31.1.01cha

Chaudhary, Shreesh Chandra. 1993. Issues on Indian English phonology: a rejoinder. *World Englishes* 12: 375–83. DOI:10.1111/j.1467-971X.1993. tb00035.x

Chhangte, Lalnunthangi. 1986. A preliminary grammar of the Mizo language. Unpublished MA thesis, University of Texas at Arlington.

Chodroff, Eleanor, and Colin Wilson. 2017. Structure in talker-specific phonetic realization: covariation of stop consonant VOT in American English. *Journal of Phonetics* 61: 30–47. DOI:10.1016/j.wocn.2017.01.001

Coelho, Gail. 1997. Anglo-Indian English: a nativized variety of Indian English. *Language and Society 26*: 561–89. DOI:10.1017/S0047404500021059

Das, Shyamal. 2001. Some Aspects of the prosodic phonology of Tripura Bangla and Tripura Bangla English. Unpublished PhD dissertation, CIEFL.

Datta, Sunanda. 1972–3. The pronunciation of English by Bengali speakers. *CIEFL Bulletin* 9: 35–40.

Dauer, Rebecca M. 1983. Stress-timing and syllable-timing reanalyzed. *Journal of Phonetics* 11: 51–62. DOI:10.1016/S0095-4470(19)30776-4

Davis, Katharine. 1995. Phonetic and phonological contrasts in the acquisition of voicing: voice onset time production in Hindi and English. *Journal of Child Language 22*: 275–305. DOI:10.1017/S030500090000979X

Davis, Katharine, and Mary E. Beckman. 1983. Production and perception of the voicing contrast in Indian and American English. *Working Papers of the Cornell Phonetics Laboratory 1*: 77–90. https://conf.ling.cornell.edu/plab/paper/wpcpl1-Davis.pdf

Docherty, Gerard J. 1992. *The Timing of Voicing in British English Obstruents*. Berlin, New York: Foris Publications.

Domange, Raphaël. 2011. Proficiency, language use and the debate over nativeness. Masters Degree Project, Stockholms Universitet.

Domange, Raphaël. 2015. A language contact perspective on Indian English phonology. *World Englishes 34*: 533–56. DOI:10.1111/weng.12162

Domange, Raphaël. 2020. Variation and change in the short vowels of Delhi English. *Language Variation and Change 32*: 49–76. DOI: 10.1017/S0954394520000010

Dyrud, Lars O. 2001. Hindi-Urdu: Stress accent or non-stress accent? Unpublished MA Thesis. University of North Dakota.

Eckert, Penelope. 2019. The limits of meaning: social indexicality, variation, and the cline of interiority. *Language 95*: 751–76. DOI: 10.1353/lan.2019.0072

Emeneau, Murray B. 1956. India as a linguistic area. *Language 32*: 3–16. DOI: 10.2307/410649

Filppula, Markku, Juhani Klemola, and Heli Paulasto, eds. 2009. *Vernacular Universals and Language Contacts: Evidence from Varieties of English and Beyond*. New York: Routledge.

Flege, James Emil. 1991. Age of learning affects the authenticity of voice-onset time (VOT) in stop consonants produced in a second language. *The Journal of the Acoustical Society of America 89*: 395–411. DOI:10.1121/1.400473

Flege, James Emil, Murray J. Munro, and Ian R. A. MacKay. 1995. Factors affecting strength of perceived foreign accent in a second language. *The Journal of the Acoustical Society of America 97*: 3125–34. DOI:10.1121/1.413041

Fuchs, Robert. 2013. Speech rhythm in educated Indian English and British English. Unpublished PhD dissertation, University of Münster.

Fuchs, Robert. 2015. You're not from around here, are you? – a dialect discrimination experiment with speakers of British and Indian English. In Elisabeth Delais-Roussaire, Mathieu Avanzi, and Sophie Herment, eds., *Prosody and Language in Contact: L2 Acquisition, Attrition and Languages in Multilingual Situations*. Berlin: Springer, 123–48.

Fuchs, Robert. 2018. Pitch range, dynamism and level in postcolonial varieties of English: A comparison of Educated Indian English and British English. *Proceedings of the 9th Speech Prosody*, 893–7. www.isca-speech.org/arch ive/SpeechProsody_2018/pdfs/167.pdf

Fuchs, Robert. 2019. Almost [v]anishing: the elusive /v/-/w/ contrast in educated Indian English. In Sasha Calhoun, Paola Escudero, Marija Tabain and Paul Warren, eds., *Proceedings of the 19th International Congress of Phonetic Sciences*, 1382–6. https://assta.org/proceedings/ICPhS2019/papers/ICPhS_1431.pdf

Fuchs, Robert, and Olga Maxwell. 2015. The placement and acoustic realisation of primary and secondary stress in Indian English. *18th International Congress of Phonetic Sciences*, 1–5. http://hdl.handle.net/11343/197933

Gargesh, Ravinder. 2004. Indian English: Phonology. In Edgar Schneider, Kate Burridge, Bernd Kortmann, Rajend Mesthrie and Clive Upton, eds., *Varieties of English*. Berlin, New York: Mouton de Gruyter, 992–1002.

Gargesh, Ravinder. 2008. Indian English: Phonology. In Rajend Mesthrie, ed., *Varieties of English 4*. Berlin, New York: Mouton de Gruyter, 231–43.

Ghosh, Tanmoy. 1996. Some aspects of vowel phonology in Bangla and Bangla English. Unpublished PhD dissertation, CIEFL.

Gour, Neelum Saran. 2010. Angrezi, Angrezier, Angreziest. In Makarand Paranjape and G. J. V. Prasad, eds., *Indian English and 'Vernacular' India*. Delhi: Dorling Kindersley (India), 115–18.

Government of India. 2011. *Census Results*. http://censusindia.gov.in/2011-Common/CensusData2011.html. Accessed 2020/11/18.

Grabe, Esther, and Ee Ling Low. 2002. Durational variability in speech and the rhythm class hypothesis. In Carlos Gussenhoven and Natasha Warner, eds., *Papers in Laboratory Phonology 7*. The Hague: Mouton de Gruyter, 515–46.

Gumperz, John J. 1982. *Discourse Strategies*. Cambridge: Cambridge University Press.

Gurubasave-Gowda, K. S. 1972. *Ao-Naga Phonetic Reader*. Mysore: Central Institute of Indian Languages (CIIL).

Hayes, Bruce, and Aditi Lahiri. 1991. Bengali intonational phonology. *Natural Language and Linguistic Theory* 9: 47–96. DOI:10.1007/BF00133326

Hickey, Raymond. 1986. Possible phonological parallels between Irish and Irish English. *English World-Wide* 7: 1–21. DOI:10.1075/eww.7.1.02hic

Hohenthal, Annika. 2003. English in India: loyalty and attitudes. *Language in India* 3. www.languageinindia.com/may2003/annika.html

Hundt, Marianne, and Devyani Sharma, eds. 2014. *English in the Indian Diaspora*. Amsterdam, Philadelphia: Benjamins.

Imani, Siddika, Parismita Sarma, and K. Samudravijaya. 2019. Automatic identification of native language from spoken English. *24th International Symposium Frontiers of Research in Speech and Music*, 1–6. www.iitg.ac.in /samudravijaya/publ/19nativeLangId_english_FRSM_Siddika.pdf

Iverson, Gregory K., and Joseph C. Salmons. 1995. Aspiration and laryngeal representation in Germanic. *Phonology* 12: 369–96. DOI:10.1017/S095267 5700002566

Jacewicz, Ewa, Robert Allen Fox, and Samantha Lyle. 2009. Variation in stop consonant voicing in two regional varieties of American English. *Journal of the International Phonetic Association* 39: 313–34. DOI:10.1017/ S0025100309990156

Jenkins, Jennifer. 2002. A sociolinguistically based, empirically researched pronunciation syllabus for English as an International Language. *Applied Linguistics* 23: 83–103. DOI:10.1093/applin/23.1.83

Jose, P. V. 1992. English spoken by Malayalam speakers: a phonological study with reference to source and target languages. Unpublished PhD dissertation, CIEFL.

Joshi, Shrikant, and Preeti Rao. 2013. Acoustic models for pronunciation assessment of vowels of Indian English. In *2013 International Conference Oriental COCOSDA held jointly with 2013 Conference on Asian Spoken Language Research and Evaluation (O-COCOSDA/CASLRE)*, 1–6. DOI:10.1109/ICSDA.2013.6709904

Kachru, Braj B. 1976. Models of English for the third world: white man's linguistic burden or language pragmatics? *TESOL Quarterly* 10: 221–39. DOI: 10.2307/3585643

Kachru, Braj B. 1983. *The Indianization of English*. Oxford: Oxford University Press.

Keane, Elinor. 2006. Prominence in Tamil. *Journal of the International Phonetic Association 36*: 1–20. DOI:10.1017/S0025100306002337

Keane, Elinor. 2014. Tamil intonation. In Sun-Ah Jun, ed., *Prosodic Typology 2: The Phonology of Intonation and Phrasing*. Oxford: Oxford University Press, 118–53.

Khan, Farhat. 1991. Final consonant cluster simplification in a variety of Indian English. In Jenny Cheshire, ed., *English Around the World: Sociolinguistic Perspectives*. Cambridge: Cambridge University Press, 288–97.

Khan, Sameer ud Dowla. 2014. The intonational phonology of Bangladeshi Standard Bengali. In Sun-Ah Jun, ed., *Prosodic typology 2: The phonology of intonation and phrasing*. Oxford: Oxford University Press, 81–117.

Kohli, Vijaya John. 2017. *Indian English? Reframing the Issue*. New Dehli: Pragun Publishers.

Krishna, G. Radha, and R. Krishnan. 2014. Native language identification based on English accent. *Proceedings of the 11th International Conference on Natural Language Processing*, 63–67. http://cdn.iiit.ac.in/cdn/ltrc.iiit.ac.in/icon/2014/proceedings/File22-p87.pdf

Krishna, G. Radha, and R. Krishnan. 2017. Automatic foreign accent classification of English spoken by South Indians. *International Journal of Pure and Applied Mathematics* 114: 595–604. https://pdfs.semanticscholar.org/8e2f/8331f34dff203286d69e7b47266627d9f22b.pdf

Krishna, G. Radha, R. Krishnan, and V. K. Mittal. 2018. Prosodic analysis of non-native South Indian English speech. *The 6th International Workshop on Spoken Language Technologies for Under-Resourced Languages*, 71–75. DOI:10.21437/SLTU.2018-15

Krishnamurti, Bhadriraju. 2003. *The Dravidian Languages*. Cambridge: Cambridge University Press.

Krishnaswamy, N., and Archana S. Burde. 1998. *The Politics of Indians' English*. Delhi: Oxford University Press.

Ladefoged, Peter, and P. Bhaskararao. 1983. Non-quantal aspects of consonant production: a study of retroflex consonants. *Journal of Phonetics* 11: 291–302. DOI:10.1016/S0095-4470(19)30828-9

Lalrindiki, T. F. 1989. Some aspects of the autosegmental phonology of English and Mizo. Unpublished MLitt thesis, CIEFL.

Latha, P. 1978. Intonation of Malayalam and Malayalee English: a study of comparison and contrast. Unpublished MLitt thesis, CIEFL.

Lisker, Leigh, and Arthur S. Abramson. 1964. A cross-language study of voicing in initial stops: acoustical measurements. *Word* 20: 384–422. DOI:10.1080/00437956.1964.11659830

Lombardi, Linda. 2003. Second language data and constraints on manner: explaining substitutions for the English interdentals. *Second Language Research 19*: 225–50. DOI:10.1177/026765830301900304

Maddieson, Ian. 1984. *Patterns of Sounds*. Cambridge: Cambridge University Press.

Mahanta, Shakuntala. 2001. Some aspects of Prominence in Assamese and Assamese English. Unpublished MPhil dissertation, CIEFL.

Mallikarjun, Meti. 2020. Regional languages and English: interactions and interfaces. *International Journal of Dravidian Linguistics* 49: 163–82.

Masica, Colin. 1976. *Defining a Linguistic Area: South Asia*. Chicago: University of Chicago Press.

Masica, Colin. 1991. *The Indo-Aryan languages*. Cambridge: Cambridge University Press.

Maxwell, Olga. 2014. The intonational phonology of Indian English: an auto-segmental-metrical analysis based on Bengali and Kannada English. Unpublished PhD dissertation, University of Melbourne.

Maxwell, Olga, and Janet Fletcher. 2009. Acoustic and durational properties of Indian English vowels. *World Englishes 28*: 52–69. DOI:10.1111/j.1467-971X.2008.01569.x

Maxwell, Olga, and Janet Fletcher. 2010. The acoustic characteristics of diph-thongs in Indian English. *World Englishes 29*: 27–44. DOI:10.1111/j.1467-971X.2009.01623.x

Maxwell, Olga, Elinor Payne, and Rosey Billington. 2018. Homogeneity vs heterogeneity in Indian English: investigating influences of L1 on f0 range. *Interspeech*, 2191–2195. www.isca-speech.org/archive/Interspeech_2018/

McCullough, Elizabeth A. 2013. Perceived foreign accent in three varieties of non-native English. *Ohio State University Working Papers in Linguistics* 60: 51–66.

McGilvary, George K. 2011. The Scottish connection with India 1725–1833. *Études Écossaises* 14: 13–31. https://journals.openedition.org/etudesecossaises/239

Melchers, Gunnel, and Philip Shaw. 2013. *World Englishes*. London, New York: Routledge.

Mohanan, K.P. 1992. Describing the phonology of non-native varieties of a language. *World Englishes* 11: 111–28. https://scholarbank.nus.edu.sg/handle/10635/52423

Mohanan, T., and K. P. Mohanan. 2003. Towards a theory of constraints in OT: emergence of the not-so-unmarked in Malayalee English, Available as ROA-601 from the Rutgers Optimality Archive: http://roa.rutgers.edu/view.php3?roa=601

Moon, Russell. 2002. A comparison of the acoustic correlates of focus in Indian English and American English. Unpublished MA thesis. University of Florida.

Mesthrie, Rajend, and Rakesh M. Bhatt. 2008. *World Englishes*. Cambridge University Press: Cambridge.

Mufwene, Salikoko. 2001. *The Ecology of Language Evolution*. Cambridge: Cambridge University Press.

Mukherjee, Joybrato. 2007. Steady states in the evolution of new Englishes: present-day Indian English as an equilibrium. *Journal of English Linguistics* 35: 157–87. DOI:10.1177/0075424207301888

Mukherjee, Joybrato, and Marianne Hundt, eds. 2011. *Exploring Second-Language Varieties of English and Learner Englishes: Bridging a Paradigm Gap*. Amsterdam, Philadelphia: John Benjamins.

Nagarajan, Hemalatha. 1985. Some phonetic features of Tamilian English. Unpublished PhD. Thesis, CIEFL.

Nair, N. G. 1996. *Indian English Phonology: A Case Study of Malayalee English*. New Delhi: Prestige Books.

Nair, Rami. 2001. Acoustic correlates of lexical stress in Hindi. In Anvita Abbi, R. S. Gupta, and Ayesha Kidwai, eds., *Linguistic Structure and Language Dynamics in South Asia: Papers from the proceedings of SALA XVIII round-table*. Delhi: Motilal Banarsidass, 123–43.

Nihalani, P., R. K. Tongue, and P. Hosali. 1979. *Indian and British English*. New Delhi: Oxford University Press.

Ohala, Manjari. 1999. Hindi. In *Handbook of the International Phonetic Association*. Cambridge: Cambridge University Press, 100–03.

Padwick, Annie. 2010. Attitudes towards English and varieties of English in globalizing India. Unpublished MA Thesis, University of Groningen.

Pai, Sajith. 2018. India has a new caste for native speakers only. *Quartz India*. https://qz.com/india/1198086/india-has-a-new-caste-for-native-english-speakers-only/. Accessed 2020/1/6.

Pandey, P.K. 1980. Stress in Hindustani English: A generative phonological study. Unpublished MLitt thesis, CIEFL.

Pandey, P.K. 1981. On a description of the phonology of Indian English. *CIEFL Bulletin* XVII: 11–19.

Pandey, Pramod. 2015. Indian English pronunciation. In Marnie Reed and John M. Levis, eds., *The Handbook of English Pronunciation*. Hoboken, NJ: John Wiley and Sons, 301–19.

Patil, Umesh, Gerrit Kentner, Anja Gollrad, Frank Kügler, Caroline Féry, and Shravan Vasishth. 2008. Focus, word order, and intonation in Hindi. *Journal of South Asian Linguistics*, *1*: 1–21. https://ojs.ub.uni-konstanz.de/jsal/index.php/jsal/article/view/3

Payne, Elinor, and Olga Maxwell. 2018. Durational variability as a marker of prosodic structure in Indian English(es). *9th International Conference on Speech Prosody at Poznań, Poland*, 69–73. www.isca-speech.org/archive/SpeechProsody_2018/pdfs/235.pdf

Peng, Long, and Jean Ann. 2001. Stress and duration in three varieties of English. *World Englishes* 20: 1–27. DOI:10.1111/1467-971X.00193

Phull, Disha Kaur, and G. Bharadwaja Kumar. 2016. Investigation of Indian English speech recognition using CMU Sphinx. *International Journal of Applied Engineering Research* 11: 4167–74.

Pickering, Lucy. 1999. An analysis of prosodic systems in the classroom discourse of native speaker and nonnative speaker TAs. Unpublished PhD dissertation, University of Florida, Gainesville.

Pickering, Lucy, and Caroline Wiltshire. 2000. Pitch accent in Indian-English teaching discourse. *World Englishes 19*: 173–83. DOI:10.1111/1467-971X.00167

Prince, Alan. 1990 Quantitative consequences of rhythmic organization. *Papers from the 26th Meeting of the Chicago Linguistic Society*, 355–98.

Puri, Vandana. 2013. Intonation in Indian English and Hindi late and simultaneous bilinguals. Unpublished PhD dissertation, University of Illinois, Champaign-Urbana.

Rai, Saritha. 2012. India's new 'English Only' generation. *The New York Times.* http://india.blogs.nytimes.com/2012/06/01/indias-new-english-only-gener ation/?_r=0. Accessed 2020/3/5.

Rajalakshmi, V. R. 2008. Mother-tongue interference in the English vowels of Malayali speakers of English. *International Journal of Dravidian Linguistics* 37: 215–28.

Rajendran, S., and B. Yegnanarayana. 1996. Word boundary hypothesization for continunous speech in Hindi based on F0 patterns. *Speech Communication* 18: 21–46. DOI:10.1016/0167-6393(95)00022-4

Ramus, Franck, Marina Nespor, and Jacques Mehler. 1999. Correlates of linguistic rhythm in the speech signal. *Cognition* 73: 265–92. DOI: 10.1016/S0010-0277(99)00058-X

Ravindran, N. 1974. *Angami Phonetic Reader.* Mysore: CIIL.

Ravisankar, G. 1994. *Intonation Patterns in Tamil.* Pondicherry: Pondicherry Institute of Linguistics and Culture.

Rendell, Ruth (writing as Barbara Vine). 1987. *A Fatal Inversion.* United Kingdom: Penguin.

Roach, Peter. 1982. On the distinction between stress-timed and syllable-timed languages. In David Crystal, ed., *Linguistic Controversies.* London: Edward Arnold, 73–9.

Saha, Shambu Nath, and Shyamal Kumar Das Mandal. 2017. Phonetic realization of English lexical stress by native (L1) Bengali speakers compared to native (L1) English speaker. *Computer Speech and Language* 47: 1–15. DOI:10.1016/j.csl.2017.06.006

Saha, Shambu Nath, and Shyamal Kumar Das Mandal. 2016. English lexical stress produced by native (L1) Bengali speakers compared to native (L1) English speakers: an acoustic study. *International Journal of Speech Technology* 19: 827–40. DOI:10.1007/s10772-016-9373-1

Sahgal, Anju. 1991. Patterns of language use in a bilingual setting in India. In Jenny Cheshire, ed., *English Around the World: Sociolinguistic Perspectives.* Cambridge: Cambridge University Press, 299–306.

Sahgal, Anju, and R.K. Agnihotri. 1988. Indian English phonology: a sociolinguistic perspective. *English World-Wide* 9: 51–64. DOI:10.1075/eww.9.1.04sah

Sailaja, Pingali. 2009. *Indian English*. Edinburgh: Edinburgh University Press.

Schneider, Edgar W. 2003. The dynamics of New Englishes: from identity construction to dialect birth. *Language* 79: 233–81. DOI:10.1353/lan.2003.0136

Schneider, Edgar W. 2004. Global synopsis: phonetic and phonological variation in English world-wide. In Edgar Schneider, Kate Burridge, Bernd Kortmann, Rajend Mesthrie, and Clive Upton, eds., *Varieties of English*. Berlin, New York: Mouton de Gruyter, 1111–1137.

Schneider, Edgar W. 2007. *Postcolonial English: Varieties around the World*. Cambridge: Cambridge University Press.

Scobbie, James M. 2006. Flexibility in the face of incompatible English VOT systems. In Louis Goldstein, Catherine Best, and Douglas Whalen, eds., *Laboratory Phonology 8: Varieties of Phonological Competence*. Berlin: Mouton de Gruyter, 367–92.

Shahidi, A. Hamid, and Rahim Aman. 2011. An acoustical study of English plosives in word initial position produced by Malays. *The Southeast Asian Journal of English Language Studies* 17: 23–33.

Sharma, Devyani. 2005. Dialect stabilization and speaker awareness in non-native varieties of English. *Journal of Sociolinguistics* 9: 194–224. DOI:10.1111/j.1360-6441.2005.00290.x

Sharma, Devyani. 2017. English in India. In Alexander Bergs and Laurel J. Brinton, eds., *The History of English: Volume 5: Varieties of English*. Berlin, Boston: Mouton de Gruyter, 311–29.

Sharma, Maansi. 2014. Phonological changes in the Hindi lexicon: a case of Meghalaya Hindi. In Gwendolyn Hyslop, Linda Konnerth, Stephen Morey, and Priyankoo Sarmah, eds., *North East Indian Linguistics 6*. Canberra: Asia-Pacific Linguistics, 193–212.

Shastri, S. V., 1992. Opaque and transparent features of Indian English. In Gerhard Leitner, ed., *New Directions in English Language Corpora: Methodology, Results, Software Developments*. Berlin, New York: Mouton de Gruyter, 263–75.

Shuja, Asif. 1995. *Urdu-English Phonetics and Phonology*. New Delhi: Bahri Publications.

Singh, Balbir. 2004. *An Introduction to English Phonetics*. New Delhi: Regency Publications.

Sirsa, Hema, and Melissa A. Redford. 2013. The effects of native language on Indian English sounds and timing patterns. *Journal of Phonetics 41*: 393–406. DOI:10.1016/j.wocn.2013.07.004

Sitaram, Sunayana, Varun Manjunatha, Varun Bharadwaj, Monojit Choudhury, Kalika Bali, and Michael Tjalve. 2018. Discovering canonical Indian English accents: a crowdsourcing-based approach. *Proceedings of the Eleventh International Conference on Language Resources and Evaluation*, 2876–81. www.aclweb.org/anthology/L18-1455.pdf

Sonderegger, Morgan, Jane Stuart-Smith, Thea Knowles, Rachel Macdonald, and Tamara Rathcke. 2020. Structured heterogeneity in Scottish stops over the twentieth century. *Language* 96: 94–125. DOI:10.1353/lan.2020.0003

Steriade, Donca. 2000. Paradigm uniformity and the phonetics-phonology boundary. In Michael Broe and Janet Pierrehumbert, eds., *Papers in Laboratory Phonology*. Cambridge: Cambridge University Press, 313–34.

Sridhar, Kamal K. 1989. *English in Indian Bilingualism*. New Delhi: Manohar Publications.

Stuart-Smith, Jane, Morgan Sonderegger, Tamara Rathcke, and Rachel Macdonald. 2015. The private life of stops: VOT in a real-time corpus of spontaneous Glaswegian. *Laboratory Phonology* 6: 505–49. DOI:10.1515/lp-2015-0015

Trudgill, Peter. 2004. *New-Dialect Formation: The Inevitability of Colonial Englishes*. Edinburgh: Edinburgh University Press.

Trudgill, Peter, Daniel Schreier, Daniel Long, and Jeffrey P. Williams. 2004. On the reversibility of mergers: /W/, /V/ and evidence from lesser-known Englishes. *Folia Linguistica Historica* 24: 211–33.

Van Els, Theo, and Kees De Bot. 1987. The role of intonation in foreign accent. *The Modern Language Journal* 71: 147–55. DOI:10.2307/327199

Van Rooy, Bertus. 2011. A principled distinction between error and conventionalized innovation in African Englshes. In Joybrato Mukherjee and Marianne Hundt, eds., *Exploring Second-Language Varieties of English and Learner Englishes*. Amsterdam, Philadelphia: John Benjamins Publishing Company, 189–207.

Vaux, Bert, and Bridget Samuels. 2005. Laryngeal markedness and aspiration. *Phonology* 22: 395–436. DOI:10.1017/S0952675705000667

Vijayakrishnan, K. G. 1978. Stress in Tamilian English: a study within the framework of generative phonology. Unpublished MLitt thesis, CIEFL.

Wells, J.C. 1982. *Accents of English*. Cambridge: Cambridge University Press.

Wiltshire, Caroline R. 2005. The "Indian English" of Tibeto-Burman language speakers. *English World-Wide* 26: 275–300. DOI:10.1075/eww.26.3.03wil

Wiltshire, Caroline. 2014. New Englishes and the emergence of the unmarked. In Eugene Green and Charles Meyer, eds., *The Variability of Current World Englishes*. Berlin, New York: Mouton de Gruyter, 13–40.

Wiltshire, Caroline. 2015. Dravidian varieties of Indian English. In G.K. Panikkar, B. Ramakrishna Reddy, K. Rangan and B.B. Rajapurohit, eds., *Studies on Indian Languages and Cultures*. Thiruvananthapuram: International School of Dravidian Linguistics, 49–63.

Wiltshire, Caroline. 2017. Emergence of the unmarked in Indian Englishes with different substrates. In Markku Filppula, Juhani Klemola and Devyani Sharma, eds., *The Oxford Handbook of World Englishes*. Oxford: Oxford Press, 599–620.

Wiltshire, Caroline R., and James D. Harnsberger. 2006. The influence of Gujarati and Tamil L1s on Indian English: z preliminary study. *World Englishes 25*.1: 91–104. DOI:10.1111/j.0083-2919.2006.00448.x

Wiltshire, Caroline, and Russell Moon. 2003. Phonetic stress in Indian English vs. American English. *World Englishes 22*.3: 291–303. DOI:10.1111/1467-971X.00297

Acknowledgments

I thank my collaborators and research assistants on previous and ongoing work on IndE, especially Pamir Gogoi for help collecting sound files for this Element despite the COVID-19 pandemic. Thanks also to Cambridge Elements Series Editor Edgar Schneider, Editorial Assistant Isabel Collins, and to the anonymous peer reviewers for their helpful questions and suggestions. Any errors remaining are my own.

Cambridge Elements $\equiv$

World Englishes

Edgar W. Schneider
University of Regensburg
Edgar W. Schneider is Professor Emeritus of English Linguistics at the University of Regensburg, Germany. His many books include *Postcolonial English* (Cambridge, 2007), *English around the World, 2e* (Cambridge, 2020) and *The Cambridge Handbook of World Englishes* (Cambridge, 2020).

About the Series
Over the last centuries, the English language has spread all over the globe due to a multitude of factors including colonization and globalization. In investigating these phenomena, the vibrant linguistic sub-discipline of "World Englishes" has grown substantially, developing appropriate theoretical frameworks and considering applied issues. This Elements series will cover all the topics of the discipline in an accessible fashion and will be supplemented by on-line material.

Cambridge Elements ⹀

World Englishes

Elements in the Series